SO-AFR-762

WITHDRAWN
DOWNERS GROVE PUBLIC LIBRARY

Griefstruck:
When a Death Changes Your Life

A personal journal
for coping with loss

All the best,
Marguerite O'Connor

Mary Ann Greene, M.P.S., M.S., LPC
and
Marguerite O'Connor, M.Ed., LFD

www.Griefstruck.com

authorHOUSE™

1663 LIBERTY DRIVE, SUITE 200
BLOOMINGTON, INDIANA 47403
(800) 839-8640
WWW.AUTHORHOUSE.COM

This book is a work of non-fiction. Unless otherwise noted, the author and the publisher make no explicit guarantees as to the accuracy of the information contained in this book and in some cases, names of people and places have been altered to protect their privacy.

© 2005 Mary Ann Greene, M.P.S., M.S., LPC and Marguerite O'Connor, M.Ed., LFD. All Rights Reserved.

No part of this book may be reproduced, stored in a retrieval system, or transmitted by any means without the written permission of the authors.

First published by AuthorHouse 03/29/05

ISBN: 1-4208-1126-6 (e)
ISBN: 1-4208-1125-8 (sc)

Library of Congress Control Number: 2005902591

Printed in the United States of America
Bloomington, Indiana

This book is printed on acid-free paper.

Original Artwork by Kari Sieb
Photographs by GrieForum, LLC

Dedications

We are grateful to the many people who have both supported and inspired us in the development of this project -- our families, teachers, mentors, colleagues, students, clients, and friends. The generosity with which they have shared their stories has given us an unparalleled appreciation for the "telling of the tale." With their help we have learned that it is the journey itself, and not the final destination, which brings healing.

Thus we wish you well as you begin, or continue, your personal journey through grief. It is our intention that like signposts along the road, the information presented in this journal will serve to guide, direct, educate, encourage, inform, and uplift you as you embark on this journey of growth and self-discovery.

-Mary Ann & Marguerite

Table of Contents

How to use this "bereavnal"

In our work with grieving individuals and families, we have found that among their top priorities are the desire to gather relevant information and the need to express their personal thoughts and feelings. It is with this in mind that we have designed this bereavnal© – a unique combination of bereavement education and journaling opportunities. It is our hope that you will find it helpful to use this journal as a tool to help navigate your own grief path. For whether you are new to the grief process, or have been grieving for some time, you probably already have discovered one of the most basic truths about grief – grief is personal. No two people experience grief in quite the same way. There is no right way to grieve. There is no timetable. There are no rules.

Thus we have created a resource that will give you the opportunity to personalize your grief journey. One which will allow you to go at your own pace, feel what you feel, be where you need to be, for as long as you need to be there. We have included journal pages to use to reflect and record your own thoughts and feelings. Use the pages to explore your emotions, to think out those issues you may have been struggling with, to express the thoughts you may not be ready or willing to share with others yet, to tell your tale – in your own words, in your own way, in your own time.

You will see that we also have included practical information, personal experiences, questions to think about, exercises you may want to try, and occasionally, even action items. They are there to help, encourage, inspire, and educate you. We hope that you will find all of them of value, however, please keep in mind, that on this journey, you are always in the driver's seat. If an exercise doesn't feel right, skip it. You may want to come back to it at a later time. Work at a pace that is challenging, but comfortable. Take as much time as you need with each activity – work when you feel up to it, rest when you feel the need.

Regardless of whether your loss was sudden or expected, recent or in the past, how you cope is now up to you. Whether you will allow yourself to be defeated by your loss, or grow stronger in its pain, is up to you. You may never have imagined yourself in this circumstance or anticipated this turn of events- but here you are - at the end of one journey, and the beginning of another.

NOTE: This book is not intended to be used as a replacement or substitute for professional medical care or mental health counseling and support. If you are struggling with a significant issue related to your loss, or are experiencing severe or prolonged medical symptoms, please seek professional help to monitor your individual situation and behaviors. If you are currently working with a counselor, or are participating in a support group, you may wish to incorporate your journaling into your discussions or use this book as a supplemental guide.

We must be
willing to get
rid of the life
we've planned,
so as to have
the life that is
waiting for us.

-Joseph Campbell

A note from the authors...

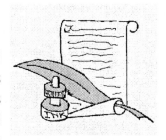

Welcome fellow traveler. We feel privileged to join you on one of life's most challenging and sacred journeys – a journey of loss and grief – and yet, hopefully a journey of growth and reconciliation. This journey will not always be easy. Most likely, there will be moments of pain, tears, and perhaps even seemingly inconsolable sadness.   But know that there will also be moments of hope, joy, and triumph.

In this book, you will find frequent travel metaphors as, in many regards, the grief journey is a virtual road trip. Like any journey, it has a fixed starting point in that it often begins with the death of someone you love. And like most trips, the grief journey also is dynamic in nature for it presents an ever-changing landscape filled with challenges and opportunities.

Your world has been changed, forever, by your loss. You may be feeling sad, tired, disoriented, or overwhelmed. Or perhaps you are feeling that you are coping well with your loss and yet at times find yourself wondering why you are unable to make a decision, complete a project, maintain relationships, or enjoy simple pleasures. The road ahead may seem unfamiliar and uncertain. For now, know that there is real power in embracing this moment, in being where you are, and in seeing yourself in the driver's seat.

The road ahead...

Right now, what lies ahead may feel unpredictable,   lonely, and even frightening. We hope it will be of some comfort to know that many have traveled the road before you. In fact, most of us have experienced loss in various forms in our lifetime. Though everyone's experience with loss is unique, there are also similarities.

In each chapter, along with information about the grieving process, you will find the words and experiences of those who have known the grief of losing a loved one. Whether they have experienced the loss of a child, spouse, parent, sibling, or close relative, they have shared their stories in hopes of providing some comfort and hope. We, too, have shared some of our experiences with loss as well as some of our professional encounters with grieving people. We have done so for it has been through our own grief as well as our work with grieving families that we have learned much of what it means to be "griefstruck", a term we are using to describe those moments when the reality of one's loss is inescapable. When people are griefstruck they may find themselves overcome with emotion, confronted by the reality of their loss, and acutely aware that their lives and relationships will never be the same.

In these griefstruck moments, grieving people may experience a sense of thinking, feeling, or moving as if on autopilot – acting without conscious awareness. They may repeat familiar patterns or habits. For example, without thinking, a widow may set a place for her late husband at the dinner table, a bereaved daughter may pick up a phone to share good news with her deceased mother, or grieving parents may automatically drive to school to pick up their child, only to discover that in the midst of these actions, the reality of their loss will come rushing back. People who are griefstruck also may experience a sudden burst of emotion when it is least expected or wanted, such as at a family celebration or as one completes daily tasks. Additionally, people may be thought of as griefstruck any time they are confronted with the reality that the loss is permanent, their vision of the future is altered, and their relationships with friends and family are forever changed.

Chapter One: The Journey Begins

You are here.

Oftentimes when a death occurs the initial reaction may be shock or denial. Whether the loss was sudden and traumatic, or slow and anticipated, there is a moment in which one realizes there is no going back, there is no opportunity to change what has occurred for the loss is now permanent. While the immediacy of a death may make the pain seem almost unbearable, ultimately there is relief as one grieves.

As you begin or continue your grief journey, you may find it helpful to understand more about the grief process, where you stand in it, and its current impact on your life. Throughout this bereavnal you will find information about the grief process -- why one grieves, what happens physically and emotionally when one is grieving, and what types of things help or hinder one's grief work. Also, in each chapter you will find the real world experiences of grieving people who have graciously shared their stories, in their own words, to offer comfort, inspiration, and hope.

You will discover in the experiences of others that no matter how disoriented you are feeling and, no matter how deep your sorrow, what you are feeling today is not permanent. The nature of grief is that it is transitory. Its purpose is to help you acknowledge your loss, and through the gradual acceptance of it, find a way to adjust to life without your loved one. Aspects of your pain, your sadness, your grief will remain with you; however, for most people, the intensity will lessen with time.

You may ask "how much time?" Bereaved people often want to know "When will this pain stop? When will I feel like myself again? When will I be able to laugh or feel joy again? Is what I am feeling normal?" For most of us, there are answers to

1

those questions. And perhaps that is one of the greatest gifts of this bereavnal, for as you record your thoughts, feelings, wishes, hopes, and dreams, you will begin to discover those answers for yourself. You will be able to see where you started, where and how you have changed, and where you still may need or want to grow. So as you begin this journey of growth and self-discovery, take a few minutes to record where you are today, and what you hope will most change as you move through your grief.

At the time of my loss I was overwhelmed by feelings of grief, guilt, and vulnerability.

-H.G.
Son whose father completed suicide

Today I ...

Look like this:

Feel like this:

Express yourself: Use creativity to express your feelings. You may use photographs, draw stick figures, cut out magazine images, write key words or phrases, or use colored markers to represent your thoughts and feelings.

_____

_____

_____

_____

_____

_____

_____

_____

_____

_____

_____

_____

_____

_____

_____

_____

_____

_____

_____

_____

_____

_____

_____

At the time of my loss I remember actually being outside of my body and thinking, I didn't know that I would feel actual physical pain. My nerves felt totally shot – almost as if the nerve endings were exposed and raw.

-M.K,
Mother whose daughter died in 9/11/01 tragedy

Well has it been said that there is no grief like the grief which does not speak.

-Henry Wadsworth Longfellow

_____

_____

_____

_____

_____

_____

_____

_____

_____

_____

_____

_____

_____

_____

_____

_____

_____

_____

_____

_____

_____

_____

Checkpoint

Many people experience physical changes in their body or daily routines during the grief process. Some people experience headaches, back or stomach pains, lack of energy, even muscle fatigue or weakness. Others experience a change in appetite, sleeplessness, or the desire to sleep too much.

What changes, if any, have you noticed?

In your body

_____

_____

In your daily routine

_____

_____

In your appetite

_____

_____

In your sleep patterns

_____

_____

In your overall health

_____

_____

Tip: Remember, experts suggest a medical check-up following a significant loss. Consult your doctor if you experience severe or persistent symptoms.

_____

_____

_____

_____

_____

_____

_____

_____

_____

_____

_____

_____

_____

_____

_____

_____

_____

_____

_____

_____

_____

_____

Despite my mother's illness, I was unprepared for her death. I foolishly thought that I would be at peace because I did not want her to suffer. However, I did not receive any comfort when she finally passed. I just wanted her back and healthy.

-K.O'C.
Daughter whose mother died of congestive heart failure

Why you grieve . . .

To understand the value of grieving, it may be necessary to first review some basic definitions. According to bereavement professionals, grief is commonly defined as an internal, emotional response to an external event of loss. Mourning, on the other hand, is grief you share with others. It is an external, shared social response which may help you adjust to your loss with the support of others.

There is value in both mourning and grieving the loss of your loved one. Often the healing power of grief begins with the funeral or memorial service. As difficult as it is for family members and friends to identify or view the deceased, the process does help those involved accept the reality of the death. Think of the tragedy of family members who do not have the opportunity to say this final good-bye to their loved one. As one often hears in news stories, people in these situations frequently may find it more difficult to acknowledge their loss, as a part of them (even at times a very small part) continues to hope that perhaps their loved one is still alive. Of course, while many people wish that they had the opportunity to continue to hold out hope for a loved one to be returned to them, the reality is that often grief work does not begin until it is acknowledged and accepted that a loss has occurred.

As the reality of the loss is accepted, one gradually moves from an intellectual to an emotional response. As the shock of the death, which is often described as a numb feeling, begins to give way, one begins to feel the pain of the loss. While this often is a difficult process, avoidance of the pain, either through one's denial or unhealthy coping mechanisms, simply delays the inevitable or often adversely affects one's physical and emotional well-being.

The loss of a loved one may result in new roles, responsibilities, and relationships. New relationships may be formed while others may fade away as the bereaved learns to adapt to new circumstances. As one redefines his or her personal identity, new challenges and barriers may develop. Financial responsibilities, household chores, and child-rearing roles within the family may be shifted. Also as new relationships are formed, feelings of guilt, fear, or betrayal may complicate the process as the bereaved individual struggles to let go of the physical presence of a loved one while preserving his or her memory.

People grieve because they are human. They form relationships. They love, and when they are denied that love through loss or death, they may feel cheated, abandoned, angry, and they grieve. Grief may temporarily insulate us from others and force us to slow down, reflect, and turn inward. Ideally, as one does so, one is given the time, opportunity, and support to integrate a new identity and learn to live with his or her loss. However in today's culture, the reality is that one is often expected to "get over" one's loss; unhealthy messages such as this may inhibit grieving, or force a person to grieve in isolation.

When a loss occurs, grief is inevitable; yet, how one grieves does make a difference. While this workbook will not be able to take the pain out of your grief journey, hopefully the tips, tools, techniques, and personal experiences offered will be able to help you find meaning in your grieving.

It helped that others let me cry, let me talk and assured me that the intense pain would cease in time.

- P.M.
Bereaved mother

I was surprised at how difficult my father's death was for me. I was an adult and he had lived a good, full life. There were blessings in his death, yet his absence left me incredibly sad.

-D.G.
Daughter whose father died at age 77

_____

_____

_____

_____

_____

_____

_____

_____

_____

_____

_____

_____

_____

_____

_____

_____

_____

_____

_____

_____

_____

_____

_____

_____

_____

_____

_____

_____

_____

_____

_____

_____

_____

_____

_____

_____

_____

_____

_____

_____

_____

We are a family of five that has learned to live as a family of four.

-N.M.
Mother whose son died of Sudden Infant Death Syndrome

The Value of Ritual

One of the most universal ways to express grief is through personal and public ritual. A ritual may be any ceremony with symbolic content. Ceremonies fill human needs of establishing order, marking significant events, communicating meaning, facilitating bonding, and coping with challenges and mysteries. They establish order by giving us prescribed guidelines which can be comforting in times of high emotion and stress; rituals help us bring order to chaos.

Rituals are used to mark significant events such as birth, rites of passage, marriage, and of course, death. Healthy rituals help us through these life transitions by giving us a focus for our thoughts and feelings. They help us remember and honor people and events. Rituals communicate meaning; they affirm what has happened in the past, document what is happening in the present, and connect us to the future. Rituals create bonds by bringing individuals together into a group with a common purpose. You may share food, drink, memories, remembrances, and customs in a caring, compassionate, and supportive way.

Rituals also help bring us into a spiritual encounter; the combination of group energy, food, music, and interaction can move us to a higher level of connectedness and communication with each other and a Higher Power. Often rituals inspire us to do a self-inventory, to focus on the meaning of our lives, and to celebrate our interconnectedness. Without ritual, people may feel more alone, isolated, and disconnected from others.

What is the value of death rituals?

- emotional support

- an opportunity to give and receive love

- a way to honor the person who died

- a means of saying goodbye to the deceased

- a chance to recall shared memories

- a recognition of our inter-connectedness

- validation of a life lived

- expression of hope and faith in the future

Remembering and Celebrating

If a memorial service was held for your loved one, hopefully you found it to be both comforting and meaningful. However, you may find that you still would like to design a personal ritual to remember and celebrate the life of your loved one. What will bring you and your family comfort now? For example:

- Create a basket of remembrance or memory box into which you place items that remind you of the person; these items may be letters, poems, notes, photographs or personal items (any connection to the person who died such as jewelry, clothing, awards, wallet, etc.).

- Light a candle or incense, pray, read poems, play music.

- Visit the cemetery or a place that feels meaningful or sacred.

- Make a donation, a gift of money or your time, to a charity or organization in honor of your loved one.

- Wear a commemorative ribbon, pin, or piece of jewelry.

- Complete a photo album or scrapbook celebrating your loved one's life and times.

- Create holiday rituals which will remember and honor your loved one.

- Start a memorial fund or scholarship.

- Dedicate a space in your home or garden to honor and remember your loved one.

- Design a family tradition, ritual, or website which can be shared with others to commemorate your loved one.

_____

_____

_____

_____

_____

_____

_____

_____

_____

_____

_____

_____

_____

_____

Griefstruck

When I was a young child, my sister, Angela, died shortly after her birth. For years, my siblings and I never talked about her at the holidays, for fear of hurting our parents. One holiday, my sister gave each family member a handkerchief angel, along with our parents' remembrances of Angela's birth and death. Rather than stirring painful memories, we have found that each season as we put our special angel on our own tree, and read the story of our sister's short life, we are able to feel more connected to her and each other.   -M.A.G.

_____

_____

_____

_____

_____

_____

_____

_____

_____

_____

_____

_____

_____

_____

_____

_____

_____

_____

_____

_____

_____

_____

_____

You expect to have to bury your parents, but never your child.

-R. T.
Mother whose 18-year old son died in a car accident

R Factor: Relationships and Grief

Our relationships are powerful influences in our lives. They can be a source of happiness, success, and support as well as a source of sadness, disappointment, and stress. They help define us, and add meaning and purpose to our thoughts, feelings, and actions.

Relationships are formed throughout our lives. Some relationships are inherited at birth; others are chosen. Some are short-lived; others last a lifetime. However, all relationships have one thing in common, they change. Sometimes the changes are welcomed as relationships grow and mature; other times, changes are unwelcome or unexpected.

The kaleidoscope of loss

Just as the bits of colored glass in a kaleidoscope reflect beautiful patterns, your relationships frequently reflect your best qualities. In them, you often see your strengths, your hopes and dreams, and your uniqueness mirrored back to you. Thus when your relationships end, either through loss or death, you lose something valuable and you grieve. According to respected colleagues and bereavement educators, there are many factors that influence your grief. Your physical health, your emotional make-up, your coping style, your loss history, your sense of spirituality, your age, even your gender may all influence the way you experience grief.

Your life circumstances also may impact how you grieve. For example, perhaps you delayed or minimized your grief reactions at the time of your loss due to family obligations. Many bereaved people have found themselves denying their own needs in order to take care of young children, provide help to elderly parents, address financial concerns, or handle other pressing obligations. While this is a natural response, not allowing yourself the opportunity to grieve can prolong your pain and sorrow.

The loss of relationship

Other significant factors affecting how well you are able to cope with loss are your relationships – your relationship to the person who died, to yourself, to a Higher Power, to others, and even to broad concepts such as how you embrace change and accept loss. In a very real sense, your relationship to the person who died gives shape and substance to your grief experience. Were you best friends . . . life partners . . .family members. . . neighbors. . . co-workers? Did you know the person for a few months . . . years . . . decades? Did he or she play a significant role in your life? What type of things did this person do for you . . . and with you? What types of things do now have to do for yourself because this person is missing from your life? Take some time to reflect upon your relationship to the person who died.

What was the nature of your relationship (for example, spouse, parent, child, friend)?

_____

_____

_____

How close of a connection did you feel? Was the person well-liked... loved... tolerated? Did you get along most of the time... some of the time... hardly ever?

_____

_____

_____

What is your favorite memory of the person?

_____

_____

Describe a difficult time with the person.

_____

_____

How was your relationship at the time of the person's death?

_____

_____

How were you notified of the person's death?

_____

_____

What was the cause of the person's death? Do you have any unanswered questions about how, or why, the person died?

_____

_____

Are there things you still wish you could have said or done with the person before he or she died?

_____

_____

What do you miss most about this person now that he or she is missing from your life?

_____

_____

Today, three months later, we still don't have a cause of death and questions still remain. That makes it hard to focus on our loss. For me, no matter what happened my brother is dead. No explanation of events will alter that. I have an amazing lack of interest in "why." But I am unusual in my family. They are all focused on that.

_-P.B._

Honor your loss

An important step in learning to cope with your loss is honoring its impact and influence in your life. Whether you have been grieving for weeks, months, or years, your grief is part of your everyday life. How you feel, how you relate to others, how you care for yourself may all be affected by your grief. Take time, now, to reflect on your grief experience thus far. What opportunities to grieve have you given yourself?

_____

_____

_____

_____

_____

_____

_____

_____

_____

_____

_____

_____

_____

_____

_____

_____

_____

_____

_____

Great grief makes sacred those upon whom its hand is laid. Joy may elevate, ambition glorify, but only sorrow can consecrate.

-Horace Greeley

My son, Chad, died at the age of 21 as a result of suicide. His fiancée took her life 10 weeks later. This double tragedy immediately impacted my life and continues today. The greatest personal impact was the "loss of dreams." Like every parent, I looked forward to seeing my son marry, having our grandchildren, and being there for me when I grew old.

-N.Z.

If Only...

When you are griefstruck, your feelings, thoughts, and actions are often influenced by those who are there to help you, such as clergy, funeral directors, family members, medical personnel, hospice staff, and friends. After the shock and numbness lessen, you may find yourself revisiting some of the decisions you made, or replaying aspects of your final days with your loved one.

In some cases, reviewing your relationship with the person you lost may trigger surprising feelings or deep regrets. Sometimes when you are remembering your relationship, you may think if only I had another chance . . . another chance to say or do something differently . . . another chance to express your emotions . . . another chance to say good-bye. Perhaps you will find yourself regretting something you did . . . or feeling guilty about something you did not do.

While you cannot change the reality of your loss, you can recreate those moments in your mind by visualizing the experiences as you wish they had occurred. You can say all the things you wish you had said – do the things you wish you had done—make the experiences what you wish they could have been. Wishing will not change the outcome, but it may help you to identify, acknowledge, and release your feelings as well as better prepare you to cope with future losses.

Tip: Bereaved people have shared that in some cases they have found it helpful to write letters to their loved ones regarding their unresolved feelings, questions, or regrets. At some time, you may wish to write a letter or poem to your loved one to further explore your thoughts and feelings.

If I had another chance . . .

This is what I would say

_____

_____

This is what I would do

_____

_____

This is what I would change

_____

_____

This is what I wish the person knew

_____

_____

This is how I wish we had spent our final moments together

_____

_____

It is one of the most beautiful compensations of this life that no man can sincerely try to help another without helping himself.

-Ralph Waldo Emerson

Griefstruck

On the day of his funeral, Mrs. P. was walking into church behind her husband's casket. In an agitated tone, she said to her adult daughter, "Where the heck is your father?" In a flash she realized what she had said. Many bereaved people experience similar moments when they may pick up a phone, address an envelope, call out a name, or make plans only to realize that the person they were counting on "being there" is no longer with them. These moments are frequently part of the grief process and will occur less often in time.   -M.O'C.

_____

_____

_____

_____

_____

_____

_____

_____

_____

_____

_____

_____

_____

_____

_____

_____

_____

_____

_____

_____

_____

_____

_____

_____

_____

_____

_____

_____

_____

_____

_____

_____

_____

_____

_____

_____

_____

_____

_____

"You'll have to ask your Dad." I can't believe I still say that when our grown children ask me something. It just slips out. I still say it — I do — all the time.

-R. T.
Wife whose husband died recently

As I progress on my grief journey, here is what I hope to change:

About my thoughts:

_____

_____

About my feelings:

_____

_____

About my actions:

_____

_____

About my relationships:

_____

_____

About my situation:

_____

_____

_____

_____

_____

_____

_____

_____

_____

_____

_____

_____

_____

_____

_____

_____

_____

_____

_____

_____

_____

_____

_____

Many years ago when my mother died in a hospital, I felt helpless and needed to see something positive. I went to where the newborns were. It helped to see the new babies and gave me a feeling that death was part of the life process.

-T. McC.

Hearts learn by being wounded.

-Oscar Wilde

Key Insights

What have I learned about myself?

_____

_____

_____

What have I learned about my
relationship with others?

_____

_____

_____

What have I learned about my loss?

_____

_____

_____

What have I learned about my grief?

_____

_____

_____

Chapter Two: It's a Winding Road

The grief journey is never a straight road. There are many twists and turns, ups and downs, and stops and starts along the way. On any journey it is helpful to know not only where you are heading but also where you have been. It is important to acknowledge the road you have traveled because it has brought you to where you are today. You have had many experiences and learned many lessons along the way. While clichés may encourage you not to "live in the past," reflecting on your past experiences may provide valuable insights to your current thoughts and behaviors. Also these past lessons may serve as treasured reminders of just how far you have come, as well as signposts to help navigate the road ahead.

One of the most challenging aspects of the grieving process is the emotional roller coaster many people experience. Up one day, down the next. Coping well one day and struggling to get out bed another. So what is normal? While grieving people often ask this question, the bottom line is that the grief process is such a unique experience that it is often challenging to define any aspect of it as "normal" or typical. However, it may be reassuring to know that most grieving people do experience emotional highs and lows. In fact, grieving people often experience a wide range and intensity of emotion as they grieve. Acknowledging and accepting what you are feeling, and knowing that the intensity of these feelings is temporary, may help you cope with the ups and downs of your emotions.

It also may be helpful to think of grief as being tidal in nature. In fact, grief has been compared with the waves of an ocean that sometimes splash at your feet and sometimes may overwhelm you. The emotions experienced by grieving people are not simple, nor are they linear, progressing neatly from one point to the next. However, those who have experienced the grief journey know that while their grief experiences are unique, they do share commonalities with other grieving people.

Often as bereaved people share their stories they discover that they have moved through, or experienced, similar stages or phases of grief. For example, grieving people frequently experience shock or denial when they first are told of the death of a loved one. They may try to bargain away the reality of their loss, and may become angry or depressed when they cannot change or avoid the pain of the loss. Ultimately, most do learn to accept that death has changed their world, and go on to face the challenge of learning to live in a world without their loved one by their side. However, as grieving people will tell you these experiences or stages often do not occur in an orderly or predictable pattern. Some people may experience the emotions of more than one stage at a time, and others may return to an "earlier" phase as new information is received, the shock of the death begins to wear off, or deeper emotions are experienced.

Thus, it is important to acknowledge that accepting and reconciling one's grief is a process. It is a process that takes time . . . takes work . . . and takes courage. However, the result is well worth the effort for as one reconciles his or her grief, the door is opened, once again, to experience the fullness of life.

I still miss her terribly and my eyes tear up when I look at her photos. She was young, only 52, I have some pictures of her from our days together as children. I am making copies of them for her sons.

-T. McC.
On the death of his sister

Now I...

Experience emotional highs and lows

- ☐ Rarely
- ☐ Infrequently
- ☐ On occasion
- ☐ Often
- ☐ Daily

Am aware of feeling physically depleted and drained

- ☐ Rarely
- ☐ Infrequently
- ☐ On occasion
- ☐ Often
- ☐ Daily

Find it difficult to concentrate or focus on tasks

- ☐ Rarely
- ☐ Infrequently
- ☐ On occasion
- ☐ Often
- ☐ Daily

Experience emotional outbursts (tears, anger, etc.)

- ☐ Rarely
- ☐ Infrequently
- ☐ On occasion
- ☐ Often
- ☐ Daily

Feel physical discomfort- pain, headache, upset stomach

- ☐ Rarely
- ☐ Infrequently
- ☐ On occasion
- ☐ Often
- ☐ Daily

The many faces of grief

Most of us know people who also have experienced loss in their lives. When you think of people you have known who have weathered the storm of loss, whose face do you see? Do you think of a grandparent . . . your mother or father . . . a close friend? As a child did you see your grandparents experience the loss of a spouse? As an adult have you seen friends and family members through the death of a loved one? Have you helped guide your own children through the loss of a pet, a friend, a neighbor, or relative? What did these experiences teach you about the many faces of grief? Sometimes by recalling memories of past losses, helpful links to present-day feelings and beliefs are uncovered.

Take some time to recall the losses you have experienced. Also, if you have the time, look through family photos, talk with relatives, ask others about their experiences and memories of loss. As you listen be aware of the similarities and differences to your own experiences. Note the feelings and behaviors that others said helped them cope with loss as well as those that did not. This information may be helpful later as you reflect back on your own loss history.

I remember feeling numb throughout the wake and funeral service for my grandmother. I was aware of what was happening, but somehow I didn't feel as if I was really there. Weeks later, when something reminded me of my grandmother, I began to cry and felt I would never be able to stop.

-M.A.G.

_____

_____

_____

_____

_____

_____

_____

_____

_____

_____

_____

_____

_____

_____

_____

_____

_____

_____

_____

_____

_____

_____

There is a sacredness in tears. They are not the mark of weakness, but of power. They speak more eloquently than ten thousand tongues. They are the messengers of overwhelming grief, of deep contrition, and of unspeakable love.

-Washington Irving

Thinking back

Now that you have recalled the loss experiences of those closest to you, think about your own early encounters with loss. You may discover important connections to your current attitudes about life and loss.

My first experience/memory of loss was...

_____

_____

In my family, death was...

- ☐ Not discussed
- ☐ Dealt with hesitantly
- ☐ Talked about openly

Grieving was something that was...

- ☐ Done in private
- ☐ Kept within the family
- ☐ Shared with others

As a child, I thought death was...

_____

_____

As a child, I was most affected by the death of...

_____

_____

_____

_____

_____

_____

_____

_____

_____

_____

_____

_____

_____

_____

_____

_____

_____

_____

_____

_____

_____

_____

_____

_____

_____

Sometimes a person has to go back, really back – to have a sense, an understanding of all that's gone to make them-before they can go forward.

-Paule Marshall

Moving forward

My most recent experience with loss was...

_____

_____

The loss was commemorated by...

- ☐ funeral or memorial service
- ☐ private ritual
- ☐ no ceremony

I dealt with the loss by...

- ☐ keeping my feelings to myself
- ☐ sharing my feelings with family members
- ☐ talking about it with friends, co-workers, and others
- ☐ discussing with clergy, professional counselors, or medical staff

Today, I see death as...

_____

_____

My attitude toward death and loss has changed. Now I feel...

_____

_____

What I have learned from my experience with loss is...

_____

_____

_____
_____
_____
_____
_____
_____
_____
_____
_____
_____
_____
_____
_____
_____
_____
_____
_____
_____
_____
_____
_____
_____
_____

Joy is a great teacher, but so is despair. Wonder is a great teacher, but so is confusion. Hope is a great teacher, but so is disillusionment. And life is a great teacher, but so is death. To deny yourself any of these - any aspect- is not experiencing life totally.

-Leo Buscaglia

R Factor: Relationship to Loss

Have you ever stopped to think about your relationship to loss? Perhaps you have never thought about having one and yet most of us do. For just as death is part of life, so too is loss. Most likely you began experiencing losses when you were quite young. Perhaps your earliest memory of loss was a favorite toy, a cherished piece of clothing you outgrew, a beloved pet, or a childhood friendship. Or perhaps as a child, you experienced the pain of a parents' divorce, leaving your childhood home, or the death of a family member. Regardless of when your experience with loss began, it probably has continued throughout your life.

What is your loss quotient?

What losses have you experienced in your life? If you were to divide your life into decades, how many losses do you think would fall into each ten-year period? Think about the first ten years of your life, what did you grieve during that time? Now think about the next decade, and then the next up until the present day. Keep in mind that losses may occur in many forms from the loss of material possessions to one's health to a job, a relationship, a home, an opportunity, income, and even such hard to define concepts as one's sense of safety, well-being, peace, happiness, trust, or self-esteem.

Loss is a natural and inevitable part of life. It is also something that impacts every aspect of life. For many, loss is thought of as negative, something to avoid if at all possible, something that takes away something or someone of value. Oftentimes the moment of loss becomes locked in our memory. Vivid details of the moment can be recalled; the thoughts and feelings easily remembered. But is pain your only connection to loss?

Imagine your life, for a moment, without loss- without loss of any kind. Certainly some aspects of your life may immediately seem better, but what would those changes cost you? What would you have to give up or give back if loss was never part of your life? How would you be different if your loss history was suddenly erased? Would you be less tolerant of others? More career-focused? Less family-oriented? It is an interesting thought as it is often so difficult to associate our losses with anything positive, and yet positive changes do occur as a result of loss.

Each time you survive a loss, you become stronger, more resilient, more aware and more flexible. Each time you survive a loss you have the opportunity to use it to become more tenderhearted, more compassionate, and more tolerant of others. Loss is something that changes you, each experience imprints you, and often the pain of loss becomes a source of wisdom, compassion, and maturity in your life. You bring something of your cumulative loss history not only to each subsequent loss experience, but to your life experience as well. Honoring your relationship to loss is about restoring your balance – it is about acknowledging your loss history without allowing it to defeat or define you.

A world without loss

As tempting as it may sound, as you look back on your loss history, as you evaluate your own loss quotient, think how different your world would be – think how different you would be – without loss. Now take a few minutes to think about the loss quotients of family members or close friends. You probably know some people who have experienced a few losses in their lives as well as some who have endured many more. How are they different? Are you aware of changes - both positive and negative ones - that have come into their lives as the result of loss? Though the lessons learned through loss are often bittersweet, they also may be life-altering. What lessons have you learned, so far, from your relationship with loss? To get you started, here are just a few examples of lessons other grieving people have learned from their losses.

- Use time wisely. Time is limited and it should be spent intentionally.

- Appreciate family and friends – spend as much time with them as possible.

- Tell others you love them often.

- Be kind in your thoughts, words, and actions.

- Let go of things that do not matter – do not waste time and energy on things of little importance.

- Embrace life with joy, hope, and optimism.

- Share your passion with others; enthusiasm is contagious.

- Spend time doing things you value.

- Be grateful for simple pleasures.

- Laugh more and worry less.

- Do not get locked in the past or lost in the future- be fully present now.

- Make a difference – enrich the lives of others.

I learned that grief is a transition that offers enormous potential for growth.

-D.G.

Treasure Hunting

As you know, at the time of a loss, it is often difficult to find anything of value in it. However as one gains perspective, sometimes, it is easier to see how some positive changes may have come about as the result of, or sometimes in spite of, the pain of a loss. Go on your own treasure hunt, and see if you are able to find some good that has come into your life as the result of your unique loss history.

Start small

Do not start "gold-mining" with your most significant or most painful losses, you may not be ready to tackle those just yet. Instead, think of a loss that you remember, but one that is less personal or less intense than your current loss. Perhaps it is a loss from your childhood, or one that involved a neighbor, a classmate, friend, or even a public figure. Now close your eyes and imagine that you are in the place and time when you were told of the loss. Try to see, hear, and feel what you felt at the time. When you are ready, allow your imagination to move you forward in time. Now look back toward the loss you were thinking of and see, hear, or feel the connections that come up for you. Did this loss change your attitude, your thinking, your feelings, your relationships, your career plans, your hopes for the future? Take a few minutes to write about your experience.

I remember...

_____

_____

_____

_____

_____

_____

Children and Grief

As you recall your own memories of childhood loss, you may remember people who were nurturing and supportive, and who helped see you through your sadness. When a death occurs it is important to remember that the children and adolescents in the family are grieving, too.

Many excellent books have been written about helping grieving children and adolescents. If you have a grieving child or teen in your family, please take the time to look into some of the resources that are available. However, as all of us will likely encounter grieving children at some point in our lives, some of the basic guidelines for helping are outlined below.

Tips for helping grieving children

- **Provide a safe haven**. Children need to know that they can express their feelings without negative consequences. Let them know you are willing to listen and can handle their feelings.

- **Try to see eye-to-eye**. Literally, if you are talking with young children, try to be on their level. Sit on the floor, or raise them up. Use age–appropriate language, and avoid euphemisms such as "Grandpa went to sleep" which may confuse or frighten them.

- **Be honest**. It is okay to just share information that you feel is appropriate for their age level, but do not lie.

- **Be a role model**. When you feel ready, share a fun activity with the children. Let them see that you can still laugh and have fun as a sign that it is alright for them to do the same.

- **Return to normal schedules as soon as possible.** Try to keep children's schedules and routines as familiar as possible, as structure is reassuring.

- **Respect their parents' beliefs and wishes.** Before talking with grieving children, make sure you understand what their parents have told them about the loss. Support their parents' views; if they are different from yours, suggest the children talk with their parents about the issue.

- **Maintain boundaries.** Be tolerant of unusual behaviors (as long as safety is not an issue) but do not overindulge children or adolescents because they are grieving. Children may need your help to find ways to express their feelings but a total lack of discipline may only increase their sense of insecurity.

- **Give children time to grieve.** Understand that they may revisit their grief as they pass through developmental stages and life milestones.

Helping adolescents cope with loss

Adolescents often have special needs as they are no longer children, but do not have the maturity and life experiences of adults. Also, as adolescents are in the process of individuating, they may want to be comforted by the adults in their lives but reject their overtures. Be patient, keep the lines of communication as open as possible, and be understanding of adolescents' need for peer support.

The meaning of life is connected to the meaning of death... mourning is a romance in reverse. If you love, you grieve. There are no exceptions -only those who do it well and those who don't.

-Thomas Lynch

_____

_____

_____

_____

_____

_____

_____

_____

_____

_____

_____

_____

_____

_____

_____

_____

_____

_____

_____

Now I try to go to every wake or funeral of someone I know because I understand how much it means to the family for others to be there. I also talk with family members about the person they lost rather than being afraid I will upset them because now I know how much it matters to talk about and remember the person who died.

-M.K.

Reflection... Your Timeline of Loss

A recent loss can trigger feelings or memories of earlier losses which you may have forgotten, repressed, or just not thought about lately. It may be valuable to consider the connection between your loss history and what you are feeling today.

Consider the following categories. When did this loss occur? If you recall, write the year the person or pet died in the space provided. (Use additional paper if necessary.) Write the names and year of death in chronological order to the timeline on the next page.

Family	Year	Friends	Year
spouse		best friend	
significant other		neighbor	
mother		friend's relative	
father		close friend	
grandmother		acquaintance	
grandfather		mentor	
aunt		classmate	
uncle		**Other Key Relationships**	
daughter			
son		caregiver	
granddaughter		boss	
grandson		clergy	
parental figure		teacher	
step/half sibling		co-worker	
step/other		business partner	
cousin		coach	
niece/nephew		client	
family pet		other	

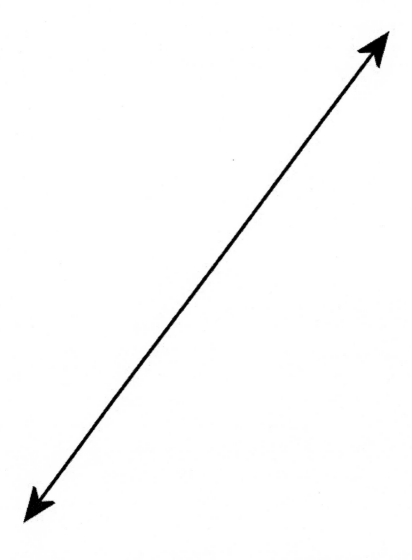

Now that you have completed the timeline, take a few minutes to reflect on your pattern of losses. When was your first loss? Your most recent loss? Do you see a cluster or pattern of losses? Did your losses occur in relationship to other significant events or illnesses? Are you aware of any major shifts in your feelings, attitudes, or outlook on life as a result of your losses? Use the following pages to reflect and review what you have learned from your loss history.

Bereavement overload is defined as too many losses occurring too quickly for the person to handle. Did this occur in your loss history?

_____

_____

_____

_____

_____

_____

_____

_____

_____

_____

_____

_____

_____

_____

_____

_____

_____

_____

_____

_____

_____

_____

_____

_____
_____
_____
_____
_____
_____
_____
_____
_____
_____
_____
_____
_____
_____
_____
_____
_____
_____
_____
_____
_____
_____
_____

Knowing that others had similar losses and survived them was helpful.

-S.N.
On the death of her 19 year old nephew in a car accident

Mourning Rituals: Yesterday vs. Today

What's different about how people grieve and mourn today? Over the last several decades, as a society, our reactions and responses to death and mourning have changed. In many cases, traditional rituals have been abandoned or replaced with more contemporary ones.

For example, previously, a person often died at home and was cared for by a personal physician and family members. Although cultural differences and preferences existed then, too, often a wreath or bunting was placed on the door, the home address was published in the death notice, and friends and neighbors brought food to comfort the grieving family. Bereaved family members often wore black clothing or armbands as a visible sign of mourning. A hearse traditionally transported the deceased to the funeral home. Funeral processions were acknowledged respectfully. Community members participated in funeral services which may have taken place over several days. Clergy and the religious congregation provided on-going support as did the extended family members who usually lived nearby. Support groups were informal gatherings of friends and family, and while family conflict existed, it was often handled within the family.

Today, a variety of medical personnel as well as professional caregivers may be used to help provide care for a dying person. Although a person still may choose to die at home, families no longer call attention to the house with funeral bunting, as personal privacy is protected and home security is now a concern. The family's address and phone number are carefully guarded and only released with the family's permission. Black clothing is so often worn that it no longer exclusively signifies mourning. A hearse may not be the only vehicle used to transport the deceased to the funeral home. Family members are geographically dispersed. Neighbors may be more isolated, and may not even know each others' names. Additionally, many people are not as closely associated with an organized religion; and therefore, at times the clergyperson conducting the funeral service may not have personally known the deceased. Funeral services are abbreviated and many choose to focus on the celebration of life. There is growing intolerance for funeral processions and some communities even have prohibited them. Today, support groups are more community-based and may even use technology (online support) to connect people who share a common grief bond. Family disputes may result in estrangement or litigation which may complicate the grieving process.

What does this mean to you? The shift away from more traditional rituals and customs may lead to a sense of isolation for some grieving people. In a world where your next-door-neighbor may not share your heritage or may be unfamiliar with your customs and beliefs, and your family may be geographically dispersed, you may need to take the first step to reach out to others. You may have to make an effort to let others know how they can best support you in your grief, what you find comforting, and how you would like others to honor the memory of your loved one. For instance, are you comfortable talking about the person who died? Is it helpful to you to discuss specific events surrounding the death, or would you prefer they not be mentioned? Do you find it reassuring or painful when others share memories of your loved one? How would you like others to remember special occasions, birthdays, and anniversaries? What changes, if any, would you like to make to holiday traditions and celebrations?

Tip: You may find that your feelings and preferences change over time. That's okay. Stay flexible. Continue to honor your own needs. Communicate your wishes to others and allow them the opportunity to provide comfort and support.

Grief will never go away. It is a part of the person you become because of your experience. The pain slowly fades and in its place are rich memories that create a relationship between you and your deceased loved one. This gives you the motivation to move forward.

_-N.Z._

Griefstruck

In the midst of a support session, a woman in her mid-50's, who had recently lost her father, began to cry. At first she just dabbed at her eyes, but soon she was openly weeping. When asked if she would like to share her feelings, she said that she had just realized that now she was an orphan. While she was much closer to her mother, who had died ten years earlier, she felt that she had not fully grieved her mother's death as she immediately began taking care of her father. Now that he was gone, too, she was feeling the impact of losing both of her parents. "Who will be there for me now" she sobbed as she expressed how alone she felt, to no longer have her parents to go to for comfort and advice.   -M.A.G.

Signposts of Grief

People are socially and culturally conditioned from the moment they are born. Girls and boys are dressed and treated differently, and their lives are shaped by certain behaviors and beliefs. There are genetic, biochemical, and psychosocial components to our behavior. These influences extend to how people grieve in that men and women often exhibit different styles of grieving. While there are always individual variations, men tend to be more cognitive and action-oriented and take a problem-solving approach to grief. They may be less comfortable being supported by others, choose not to discuss their feelings, and seek to maintain a sense of emotional "control." Widowers also may be more likely to be ready to date and even remarry sooner than widows following the loss of a spouse.

Women, on the other hand, tend to be more emotionally expressive. They may seek and be comforted by the support of family and friends. Women tend to be more open to feeling and sharing the emotional pain of grief. However as they frequently function as the emotional bedrock of a family, they also may feel the need to minimize their own grief in order to be strong for others.

In addition to gender, grief reactions are influenced by a variety of factors such as age, family dynamics, personality traits, coping skills, cultural differences and socio-economical factors. It is helpful to become aware of some of the various responses to grief in that a variety of grieving styles may exist within a family system or social group. Education, empathy, and dialogue are helpful in increasing one's understanding and tolerance for expressive differences.

Grief also may manifest in a variety of physical, emotional, and social changes. Physical symptoms may include dry mouth, headache, back pain, fatigue, muscle tightness or weakness, change in appetite, and disrupted sleep patterns. The body's immune system may be challenged by the stress of grief and may be more susceptible to colds, sore throats, and other illnesses.

Cognitive changes may be experienced in that grief disrupts our thought patterns. You may find it is more difficult to focus on reading, work, or projects. At times, you may feel confused, fearful, or befuddled. Decision-making may be difficult and even the smallest of tasks may seem overwhelming.

Also you may find that you are experiencing unfamiliar or conflicted feelings. While you miss the person, you may not miss some of his or her behaviors. You may feel abandoned by the loss of your loved ones, yet feel a sense of relief from care-giving duties and responsibilities.

Self-monitoring as well as increasing one's awareness of family members' behaviors may be helpful in evaluating the "signposts of grief." Be on the lookout for changes in familiar behaviors and patterns that may alert one to the differences between "normal" and "complicated" grief (see Chapter Three). Complicated grief often involves the need for additional support or counseling, especially when the grief reactions become incapacitating or last over a long period of time.

Why is it important to recognize when others are grieving?

It is important to know when others are grieving so that we may express caring and compassionate behaviors, and extend our condolences in a supportive way. Bereaved people want to be comforted. They often have a need to talk about the loss and to affirm that their loved one's life mattered to others. One bereaved parent shared that she always goes to funerals now, and makes a point of talking about the deceased, as she realizes how important it is for the grieving family to be able to talk about and remember their loved one.

How does one recognize a grieving person?

Today, our society is going to great lengths to protect the privacy of individuals. While in most cases this is a benefit, it does impact grieving families in that employers, religious and medical personnel, neighbors, and friends may not take responsibility for notifying others of a loss as they once did. Also as many of the outward signs that had symbolic meaning have changed, grieving people may not be as apparent today. Thus, the onus may fall to the bereaved to let others know about their loss and their need for support.

What can one do to help a grieving person?

- Provide practical assistance (offer to help with housekeeping chores, meal preparation, transportation).

- Be present; listen to the grieving person's story.

- Encourage and support use of community resources.

- Respect the person's values, customs, and beliefs.

- Stay in touch.

Cultural diversity and grief

Respecting the values, beliefs, and unique characteristics of grieving people is an important consideration. When cultural diversity intersects with grief, there is a great need for sensitivity, as emotions may be intensified. There are several ways to become more culturally aware, to have a raised consciousness and appreciation for the differences among us. One strategy is to consciously decide to understand your own culture. A deeper understanding of your values, beliefs and norms will help you recognize, take pride in, and share your own heritage. Next, take action by physically interacting with those who are different from you; be open to new experiences. For example share a meal, observe a religious service or social ritual, read a book about another culture, travel, join a business or social organization, or attend a seminar related to the topic of cultural sensitivity. There are unique traits within and between cultures. By respecting, embracing and celebrating the differences, it is easier to see that there is more that unites us, than separates us.

Gaining an appreciation for another's culture may be valuable in helping us learn how to express our sympathy in a respectful way, also. What beliefs does the culture hold regarding death and an afterlife? Which rituals and customs serve to honor the deceased? What helps survivors cope with loss? For many people, attendance and participation in funeral services is an important social obligation. Accept responsibility for teaching your children, family members, friends and neighbors about your own culture's beliefs and traditions. Invite people to teach you about their customs. Avoid stereotyping or judging; learn to appreciate and celebrate distinct aspects of cultures. Use community resources and religious leaders to expand your knowledge and recognize that cultural competency is an area of lifelong learning.

We may have come here on different boats, but now that we are here, we're all in the same boat.
-Dr. Martin Luther King, Jr.

It's amazing what you can get through when you have no choice. My neighbor, who recently lost her husband, gave me some good advice. She said, "Don't think about what might be — just take one day at a time." Now when I start thinking "what if," I stop myself and think about "what is" and somehow that makes me go on.

-D.J.S.

Checkpoint

As you reflect on other losses you have experienced such as: loss of a job, home, income, property, relationship, health, etc. think about what you may have learned from the experience.

How did the experience help you grow as a person?

_____

_____

What inner strengths or talents did you discover as a result of your loss?

_____

_____

Who helped you cope with your feelings?

_____

_____

What helped you get through the experience? (For example, listening to music, walking/exercise, prayer, talking with friends and family).

_____

_____

How did your attitude change once you recovered?

_____

_____

_____

_____

_____

_____

— _____

_____

_____

_____

_____

_____

_____

_____

_____

_____

_____

_____

_____

_____

_____

_____

_____

_____

_____

_____

_____

Sorrows are our best educators. A man can see further through a tear than a telescope.   -Lord Byron

The greatest thing in this world is not so much where we are, but what direction we are traveling.

-Oliver Wendell Holmes

_____

_____

_____

_____

_____

_____

_____

_____

_____

_____

_____

_____

_____

_____

_____

_____

_____

_____

_____

_____

_____

_____

_____

_____

_____

The past should be a springboard, not a hammock.

-Ivern Ball

_____

_____

_____

_____

_____

_____

_____

_____

_____

_____

_____

_____

_____

_____

_____

_____

_____

_____

_____

_____

_____

_____

_____

Key Insights

What have I learned about myself?

_____

_____

_____

What have I learned about my
relationship with others?

_____

_____

_____

What have I learned about my loss?

_____

_____

_____

What have I learned about my grief?

_____

_____

_____

Chapter Three: Gridlock

Just as your grief journey may not follow a predictable path, at times, you may not feel that you are moving at all. You may find yourself feeling stuck, unable to move past a particular feeling or event. Perhaps you may find yourself reliving a particular moment, remembering something you said, or did not say. Or perhaps you may find yourself continually visiting or avoiding a particular person or place because it reminds you of your loved one.

Depending on where you are in the grief process, you may find that you are experiencing a wide range of unfamiliar emotions and behaviors. Your grief responses may be looked at in terms of four broad categories: emotional, mental, physical, and social. These are offered only as a guideline, as a way of thinking and talking about your feelings, as grief reactions typically do not fall into neat, organized divisions and in fact, frequently involve more than one category.

To begin, emotional responses to grief may include a sense of feeling overwhelmed or deeply saddened. You may find that you cry more easily or express your emotions more quickly. You may feel a heightened sense of emotion or feel almost a total lack of emotion – a sense of feeling disconnected and numb. Mental or cognitive reactions may include a sense of confusion, disorientation, forgetfulness, a lack of mental clarity, and difficulty in making decisions. Physical examples include fatigue, sleep and appetite disturbances, muscle aches and pains, dryness of mouth. And finally social responses to grief may include an increased sense of isolation, loneliness, a change in family and friends, a shift in support system or social status, and renewed or estranged religious affiliations.

Although many of these feelings are part of the normal grief process and most likely will lessen in intensity, sometimes you may find that your feelings are so powerful that you feel trapped by them. In these instances, you may actually feel "stuck," unable to cope with your emotions and you may need professional help to learn to deal with them.

How do you know when you should seek professional help? A good rule of thumb is to look to the impact your feelings have on your day-to-day life. Are you able to maintain your daily routine? Do you find you are unable to sleep at night, or do you wake up feeling tired no matter how much sleep you get? Have you noticed changes in your appetite, either eating more or less than you did before you experienced your loss? Have you noticed you have stopped socializing with friends and family members because you find it too painful to be around other people? Do you find that you are overindulging with food, alcohol, drugs, or engaging in behaviors which may cause your life to become unbalanced or may be harmful to yourself or others? If you are experiencing dramatic changes in your ability to function on a day-to-day basis, seek professional help. However, if you find that you are able to function well in most areas of your life, yet feel stuck in one particular area or aspect of your grief, the following chapter will provide some self-help tips and techniques you may want to try.

In the middle of difficulty lies opportunity.
–Albert Einstein

It's ironic how things change. My son, who had always been closer to his mother, distanced himself in later years due to her alcoholic behaviors. My daughter, on the other hand, became closer as she grew older. However, both of our children found it very difficult to deal with their mother's deterioration and death. I wish there had been more time for them to resolve their feelings.

-J.O'C.
On the death of his ex-wife

Checkpoint

Are you feeling stuck in any aspect of your grief right now? Are you aware of any changes you would like to make in how you think, act, or feel? Take some time to think about how your thoughts, actions, feelings and social relationships have changed since your loss. Write down any concerns you may have, or any repetitive thoughts, feelings, or actions that you believe may be keeping you stuck.

Emotionally:

_____

_____

Mentally:

_____

_____

Physically:

_____

_____

Socially:

_____

_____

I still spend time believing that I simply haven't seen him for awhile. It's easy to fool yourself that way. He wasn't a daily presence in my life so I can generally go about my life without interruption. Then, some small thing will happen and the sadness simply overwhelms me. It's hard to imagine that I will have to continue on with the rest of my life without him.

-P.B.
On loss of adult sibling

_____

_____

_____

_____

_____

_____

_____

_____

_____

_____

_____

_____

_____

_____

_____

_____

_____

_____

_____

_____

_____

_____

Anger is always to be expected to some degree following a significant loss. It is a natural consequence of being deprived of something valued.

-Therese Rando

A frequent, normal companion of grief is anger. People often experience flashes of anger in response to situations that trigger feelings of helplessness, such as when a trust has been broken, or a loss is experienced.

Constructive anger is positive, helpful, and practical. It can convert negative emotion into positive action, and helps us destress by releasing emotional tension. Anger can also provide some protection for us. It may insulate us and thereby provide temporary relief from the reality of our loss which may allow us to experience our grief in smaller "doses." For when people are angry at others or life events, their focus becomes external, and their pain and grief may temporarily lessen. Anger also can help us establish boundaries in that it often forces people to pay attention to our intense emotions.

However, it is important to acknowledge our anger and take responsibility for it. While anger is normal, unchecked or prolonged anger also can be destructive, negative, and harmful to self and others. It can inhibit our grief and keep us stuck. Anger can become destructive when it is used to blame, intimidate, or oppress others, or when it causes us to act out of control. Anger is destructive when it hurts us, causes us to lash out at others, turns to rage, or damages relationships or property. In these extreme cases, anger management techniques or classes may be needed to learn how to safely express these powerful feelings.

Are you angry with yourself, a family member, a doctor, or someone else? Reflect on your possible sources of anger as you complete the following exercise.

I'm angry because...

I:	My family:
☐ Feel alone ☐ Feel like a failure ☐ Am not appreciated ☐ Let this happen ☐ Should have known better ☐ Other:	☐ Disappointed me ☐ Didn't help when needed ☐ Doesn't care about my feelings ☐ Wasn't there for me ☐ Doesn't understand my grief ☐ Other:
God:	**Others:**
☐ Let this happen ☐ Abandoned me ☐ Didn't protect me/my family ☐ Let me down ☐ Didn't reward my loyalty ☐ Other:	☐ Are beyond my control ☐ Say hurtful things ☐ Do not seem to care ☐ Do not acknowledge my loss ☐ Expect too much of me ☐ Other:
My loved one:	**I hold others responsible:**
☐ Died /died unexpectedly ☐ Left me with financial problems ☐ Contributed to his/her death ☐ Disregarded medical advice ☐ Experienced a violent death ☐ Other:	☐ Doctors/hospital ☐ Insurancecompanies/lawyers ☐ Mental health professionals ☐ Family members ☐ Employer/co-workers ☐ Other:

If we could read the secret history of our enemies, we should find in each man's life sorrow and suffering enough to disarm all hostility.

-Henry Wadsworth Longfellow

_____

_____

_____

_____

_____

_____

_____

_____

_____

_____

_____

_____

_____

_____

_____

_____

_____

_____

_____

_____

_____

_____

The strongest oak tree of the forest is not the one that is protected from the storm and hidden from the sun. It's the one that stands in the open where it is compelled to struggle for its existence against the winds and rains and the scorching sun.

–Napoleon Hill

Understanding your anger

Now that you have completed your anger self-inventory, think about your relationship to this powerful emotion. What makes you angry? How frequently do you get angry? How is your anger working for or against you? Do you want to change something about how you express your anger? Like all intense emotions, anger affects our thoughts, feelings, and actions. There is an interconnectedness to these three aspects of our behavior in that what one thinks about a situation will influence how one feels about it, and how one feels about a particular situation will influence how one acts.

So how do you control what you think about a situation? In some instances, our anger may be justified in that a wrongdoing against us or our loved one truly has occurred. In some cases, anger may be easier to express than hurt or sadness. And in some cases, a person may be unaware that his or her anger may be masking deeper feelings of hurt, sadness, fear, or abandonment. How do you know the difference? How do you discover whether your feelings of anger are driven by your internal emotions or external circumstances?

One consideration may be to ask whether your feelings are based on rational thinking or irrational beliefs. Look at the series of events that have taken place. Has God really abandoned you, have your friends or family members truly behaved in a hurtful way, could your emotions, or past hurts, be distorting your thinking? When in doubt, test your beliefs, challenge your thinking. Do you have factual evidence that supports your current beliefs? Do you have information which may dispute your feelings? And finally ask yourself, what do you gain by holding on to your anger, and what could you gain by letting it go?

Getting control

There is a high cost to holding on to anger. It can make you sick – physically and emotionally. It can deplete your energy and if you allow yourself to fuel your anger, it can escalate to rage. Uncontrolled anger can contaminate relationships and interfere with goals. In response to your anger, you may do and say things that you will later regret. And holding on to your anger may eventually change who you are and how you see the world.

So, when appropriate, there is value in letting your anger go, especially when you are able to release it in a safe, healthy way. Keep in mind it is natural to feel angry when you lose a loved one. You have lost something of tremendous value. Your relationship cannot be replaced, and your anger allows you to protest your loss. Your anger reflects your pain and wounded feelings, yet if you are going to continue to move through your grief, it will be helpful to learn how to control, express, and resolve your anger.

Taking charge

It's empowering to acknowledge that anger is present in your life and to take responsibility for it. For once you have recognized that you are feeling angry, the choice of how you respond to it is yours. How you respond to your anger is a matter of choice. However, it is often difficult to see your choices . . . to find options . . . when you are in the passion of the moment. Therefore it is valuable to have a series of strategies available to help to discharge or drain some of the energy out of your anger by "letting it go" in a safe manner. When you are experiencing feelings of anger, you may find it helpful to try one of the following suggestions, or experiment with your own ways of safely releasing your anger.

Letting your anger go

- Write a letter expressing your anger and then destroy it.

- Talk to an empty chair - let your feelings out.

- Hit a pillow.

- Role-play with a close friend.

- Sing your favorite song as loud as you can.

- Exercise, stretch, dance, or try Yoga postures.

- Try deep breathing exercises – breathe in to a count of three, hold for one second, then breathe out to a count of three; repeat three times.

- Progressively tighten and relax your muscles.

- Call a trusted friend or family member for support.

- Pour out your anger in a journal.

- Try aromatherapy – light scented candles or add fragrant oils to a bath.

- Spend time in nature – walk in the woods, swim in a lake, play in the snow, build a sand castle, collect shells.

- Buy something you always loved as a child, such as a new box of crayons, a paint-by-number set, an airplane model. And use it!

When anger rises, think of the consequences.
-Confucius

I still think of her all the time and feel her presence in my life. On the downside, I still harbor anger and resentment of a misdiagnosis which contributed to her death. I feel this is an unhealthy attitude, yet I can't seem to get beyond it.

-K. O'C.
Daughter whose mother died 13 months ago

_____

_____

_____

_____

_____

_____

_____

_____

_____

_____

_____

_____

_____

_____

_____

_____

_____

_____

_____

_____

_____

_____

Grief and Forgiveness

Death and dying are part of life, but coping with these issues may involve stress, disappointment, betrayal, and unmet expectations. Anger, rage, guilt and other raw emotions may surface; these powerful feelings may be directed toward a doctor, caregiver, God, family members, oneself, or even the deceased. If left unresolved, anger and resentment may be passed, consciously or unconsciously, from one generation to the next; however with effort, the cycle can be broken.

Forgiving a person for a perceived wrong does not make the offense acceptable. However, it is important for us to try to find a way to forgive those who hurt us as the alternative may result in toxic feelings which can compromise our own sense of well-being. While anger, guilt, and regret may be part of the grieving process, when they are allowed to control our actions, they can inhibit us from doing our grief work. Also, maintaining feelings of anger and resentment is a constant drain on our energy, and thus releasing them can be an act of self-care.

Releasing these negative emotions though may not be easy, especially in today's world when it seems so "normal" to hold on to our feelings of anger and resentment. Often the media coverage of a death, especially in the case of a wrongful or accidental death or one suggesting medical negligence focuses on the desire of some one to blame others. While in many of these cases there may be a real culpability, focusing on blame, to the exclusion of other feelings such as compassion, empathy, and understanding, may not only complicate the grief process, it may keep the grieving person locked in an escalating cycle of anger and resentment. In contrast, the decision to forgive, even in the face of true wrongdoing, may be one of the keys to breaking free from further loss and pain.

What it means to forgive

An important consideration when discussing forgiveness is the realization that it does not mean condoning or forgetting the actions of another. Forgiving is not excusing, pardoning (releasing from punishment or responsibility), agreeing, accepting, or justifying the actions of another. Instead forgiving is about releasing or surrendering the anger, resentment, or guilt that may keep us feeling wounded and victimized. Thus, forgiveness is an important gift to give ourselves for it allows us to release our pain and frees us from getting stuck in our own negative emotions.

The reality is that sometimes bad things do happen. One may have had no part in causing the initial pain but by refusing to forgive the offender, one may be unwittingly continuing the victimization by keeping oneself trapped in a victim's role. By refusing to stay stuck in anger and resentment, by forgiving even when the circumstances do not seem warranted, one may reclaim one's own power and sense of peace.

How to forgive

You may choose to forgive the person face-to-face, or you may prefer to work within your own frame of reference. You do not need to forgive someone in person in order for it to be effective. If you feel the other person is not open or ready to receive your forgiveness, you may want to simply resolve within yourself to let go of the situation. Or depending upon the circumstances, you may try to resolve your dispute by validating the person's importance in your life and affirming your desire to reconnect. Regardless of the situation, and regardless of the offender's response, forgiveness is a goal worth working toward. It may take effort and perseverance but ultimately, forgiveness is a way of releasing what has happened and restoring joy to one's life.

Forgiveness does not change the past, but it does enlarge the future.

-Paul Boese

_____

_____

_____

_____

_____

_____

_____

_____

_____

_____

_____

_____

_____

_____

_____

_____

_____

_____

_____

_____

_____

_____

_____

_____

Let us not look back in anger or forward in fear, but around in awareness.

-James Thurber

R Factor: Relationship to Family

Family is an important building block of society, and of our personal happiness. While legal definitions and distinctions exist, people need not be related by blood to be considered a family. Families come in all shapes, sizes and descriptions. They may be formed through marriage, partnerships, or other relationships of choice. Some families may be created through adoption, some are formed by single parents, and still others are the result of separation, divorce, or death. What matters most in defining a family is not how it originated, but the relationships that the members share.

Our connections with family members often are our longest-lasting and most influential relationships. Our families give us a common bond and a shared history. Most people seek to share happy and sad times with family members. In times of stress, it is natural to look to your family for comfort. Among the advantages of family ties are physical and social support, love and nurturing, and a feeling of connectedness. The joys and responsibilities of family often give meaning and purpose to our lives. Family bonds imprint our feelings about ourselves and teach us how to relate to others. Family interactions affect our feelings of security, safety, and trust in the world.

Family relationships may be functional, dysfunctional, or rest somewhere in-between. Within the family structure, alliances often are formed and individual members may find themselves closely connected with some members, and disconnected, or even estranged from others. Some family ties are unhealthy and can be destructive. Just thinking about family relationships might trigger physical or emotional reactions internally. Take time to think about your relationships with family and to notice any positive or negative reactions or patterns. You were born into a family that shaped who you are, and now you have the opportunity to influence and shape your family as well.

Death causes a major shift in the family. Roles, responsibilities and expectations change. Old wounds or feelings may surface, and may collide with new values and priorities. Death causes us to confront our own mortality. Experiencing a significant loss is a transformative experience; it changes us, and has the power to change our relationships with those closest to us.

Family communication

Some families have an open communication style that fosters discussion and respect. Others model patterns of closed communication with barriers such as being intolerant, judgmental, or engaging in authoritative behaviors. Sadly, these barriers and behaviors can lead to a total breakdown in communication. Sometimes, people deliberately withhold information or exclude members from decision-making. Sometimes families have secrets, and while they may have begun with good intention, such as to protect someone from hurtful information, secrets may lead to harmful behaviors.

Family support

Were you able to share your feelings with family members at the time of your loss? How did they show their support?

_____

_____

Describe your current relationship with your family.

_____

_____

What hurt were those people who said, "if there is anything I can do — and [then] disappeared from my life."

-N.Z.

Death ends a life, not a relationship.

-Morrie Schwartz

It was so hurtful when others made statements like "at least you have other children." It made me feel like they thought he didn't matter because he was so young when he died.

-P.M.
Mother whose son died when he was six months old

Messages that matter...

All of us are influenced consciously or unconsciously by subtle messages which are received from our family and the world around us. Oftentimes these verbal and non-verbal messages become internalized and shape our feelings and actions. What messages have you received from your environment that have stayed with you, and which do you think you are passing on to others?

As you complete the grid on the next page, think about the messages that you have received from your father, your mother, television programming, movies, and your cultural background about each of the topics.

Today when I think of my father, I remember all the goodness he brought to my life and all that he taught me. I am often struck by how many of his traits and characteristics are a part of who I am. When others tell me how much I remind them of my father, I am honored.

-D.G.

	Father	Mother	Media	Culture
Death				
Family				
Feelings				
Money				
Self-care				
God				

I miss my parents everyday. I miss that my daughters will never know my Dad and that neither Mom nor Dad will see what a good job I have done in raising them.

- N.M.

What Complicates Grief

Warning: Expect Delays!

When you are grieving, nothing feels "normal," yet sometimes your grief may become complicated or compounded by additional factors. As certain aspects of a loss may increase the risk of a complicated grief response, you may find it helpful to understand the term, "complicated grief" and to review examples that illustrate it. Complicated grief is a response to loss that lasts longer than normal and remains unresolved or unaccepted. The challenge in understanding the distinction between normal and complicated grief is that there is no timetable, no exact measurement of normal grief. There is no standard by which one can measure or define one person's grief as more painful or significant than another's. However, it is often helpful to view each loss, and each response to loss, in context as awareness of potential complications may help you prepare for and deal with challenges more effectively.

To begin, consider how the person died, and whether the death was sudden, unexpected, or traumatic. Sudden death may mean you had little time to prepare for the shock of death. Unexpected death also may cause you to feel distraught if you had no chance to say goodbye or were not with your loved one when death occurred. Traumatic death may cause worry that the person experienced physical or emotional pain before dying. While the age of a person is not a measurement of how much you loved them, you may feel an additional burden if you felt the person was too young to die. Or, you may feel that if you had more time, relationship issues may have been resolved. Perhaps something interrupted or interfered with your grief work, and the delay is now complicating your grief.

Unresolved grief may be the result of chronic, delayed, suppressed, distorted, or absent grief. Chronic grief exists for a long time, without lessening in intensity. Bereaved people often seek help for this because they sense that their intense grief has gone on too long, it interferes with their daily living, or a concerned friend or family member has urged intervention. Delayed grief manifests when you do not take time to grieve, are forced to postpone grieving, or when your grieving is inhibited by the use of drugs or alcohol. Perhaps you have not given yourself permission to grieve, are overscheduled, or tell yourself you cannot grieve now, and that you will do it later. Use of drugs or alcohol may numb your painful feelings but it also inhibits a conscious effort to get in touch with your emotions, and may inhibit your understanding of the grief process. Suppressed grief is hidden or contained. When you try to push something down, it often erupts when you least expect or welcome it. Distorted grief refers to that which is masking something else, or is an extreme response. For example, you may display angry behaviors when you are really wounded, or you may cry more over the death of a famous person than a close relative. And finally, absent grief means just that -- there is no grief response; you do not feel or experience any grief, just as if no death had occurred.

You may experience a complicated grief reaction as the result of:

- The death of a child. This seems to go against what is perceived to be the natural order of the universe. It is assumed that parents will die before children, not the other way around. Parents are the protectors of their children and they describe feeling defeated, guilty, or inadequate when they are not able to save their child.

- A traumatic, violent, or sudden death. These situations are often described as senseless, unfair, cruel, and unexpected. There may be secondary losses such as loss of personal property, loss of security and safety.

- A "taboo" death. Often when a death occurs as the result of homicide, suicide, addictions, or diseases that are feared, the grieving process may be complicated.

Grieving family and friends may be reluctant to share their experiences, and they may not receive the same outpouring of support as in other circumstances. There also may be secondary losses involving the criminal justice system, insurance claims, and feelings of guilt, shame or blame.

- Bereavement overload. Perhaps in the case of an isolated loss, a person is able to cope well. However, in the case of overload, several losses may occur at once, or within a short period of time. Overload also may occur when a death is compounded by other stressors, such as the loss of family connections, a home, familiar lifestyle, income, status, or security.

Understanding how these complicating factors may apply to your situation may help reduce fear or anxiety. Also, they may help you determine when professional intervention or support may be advisable. There are no simple solutions, and the healing process often takes time. It is important that you remain patient with yourself while you are grieving. Avoid excessive isolation by offering and accepting social invitations. There is a time to be alone, but also take time to be with others. Avoid self-medicating with alcohol, drugs or food. Talk with others who have had similar losses. Feeling really understood and accepted by someone is a powerful experience—and one which you can both receive and give to others. Finally, tell your story as often as you need to. As many bereaved people have shared, there is healing in the repetition.

The death of a baby is particularly traumatic as it is a disruption of the natural order. It threatens one's sense of safety.

-D.T.

Griefstruck

When our beloved grandmother, Nini, died in the middle of the night, I phoned my sister from the hospital to share the sad news. My sister let out a wail and hung up. I stood there, at the payphone, stunned. In the midst of my sorrow, I felt a flash of anger. How dare she hang up on me. I came to realize, months later, that my sister, who loves deeply, was responding in the primal way of keening. She was experiencing a griefstruck moment. It wasn't about me. It was her gut response to a painful loss.

-M.O'C.

Resolving Money Matters

When a death occurs the deep sadness and sense of loss felt by those left behind often triggers a sense of emotional vulnerability. Emotions are raw and close to the surface. Bereaved people may feel physically and emotionally exhausted. Interpersonal communication may be challenged as grieving people are stressed almost to the breaking point, and yet important decisions often must be made.

Sometimes the emotional upheaval felt following a death can express itself in terms of conflicts over money and property. Some bereaved people may find it easier to engage in a financial disagreement than to acknowledge deeper feelings. For others, financial gain may be seen as a way of righting an earlier wrong. And for still others, monetary settlements or material objects may be a way of holding on to the person they lost, or a way of comforting their own hurting hearts. Regardless of the reason, grieving people can become embroiled in conflict over property and financial issues.

What to do when conflict arises

If you find yourself in the position of "fighting" with family members, it may be helpful to step back from the conflict and ask yourself what is at the heart of your feelings. Do you feel you are being treated unfairly? Do you think caregiving or financial responsibilities were not shared or acknowledged? Do you feel entitled to a larger monetary settlement than you received? Are you feeling hurt by someone's behavior? A person who perhaps did not spend time with your loved one, did not attend the funeral, or did not honor your relationship? Do you wish that you had received an important or special item that symbolized the connection you shared with the deceased? Was there something that was special to you that was given to, or taken by, someone else?

Under the best of circumstances, answering these questions is difficult; however when you attempt to do so in the context of a grieving family, it may lead to conflict. As roles change, and economic shifts occur, long-standing issues or conflicts may surface again. One important step in resolving these conflicts is to get in touch with the feelings that may lie beneath the issue. Once you are clear on what you are feeling it will be easier to communicate it to those involved. If family members or others are not responsive, try not to be discouraged. Keep in mind that people tend to have their own style of dealing with conflict just as they do in coping with grief. Try to be sensitive if the people you are dealing with have communication styles that are different than your own. Show consideration for the people who may find it more difficult to express their feelings. Be patient with people who may not listen, or interrupt you when you are trying to express your feelings. Acknowledge that all of you have experienced a loss and are trying to cope with it.

The value of intention

Another key to resolving financial conflicts is to look to the power of intention. What is your intention in holding your ground? What do you think the intention of those you are in conflict with, may be? Could a difference in values, lifestyle, or life experiences be at the core of your conflict? Sometimes by trying to look at the issue from the perspective of the other person, and by assuming a positive intention, you may gain valuable insight into their actions as well as your own. Resolving financial conflicts often takes great diplomacy. Stay with it: express your feelings, share the meaning that things may hold for you, be open to those who may hold different values, and work toward resolution by seeking compromise. If you are unable to break through the conflict, consider seeking professional help to avoid possible litigation or estrangement from friends or family members. You have already experienced a significant loss, give yourself permission to do what it takes to resolve conflicts which may lead to additional losses.

Until you make peace with who you are, you'll never be content with what you have.

-Doris Mortman

_____

_____

_____

_____

_____

_____

_____

_____

_____

_____

_____

_____

_____

_____

_____

_____

_____

_____

_____

_____

_____

_____

_____

_____

_____

_____

_____

_____

_____

_____

_____

_____

_____

_____

_____

_____

_____

_____

_____

_____

_____

_____

_____

_____

_____

_____

Love is like a violin. The music may stop now and then, but the strings remain forever.

-June Masters Bacher

Interpersonal communication

As people begin talking at a young age, it is easy to assume that all of us should be "naturals" at communication. Professional speakers who are well-compensated will tell you that practice and preparation helped them to become skilled in polishing their message.

Communication is a powerful tool. It can be used in constructive or destructive ways.

Healthy communication can empower you, can bridge relationships, and heal wounds.

- Use "I" statements such as I feel or I think.
- Avoid judgmental words such as should, must, always, or never.
- Be aware of your non-verbal communications... gestures, facial expressions, body language, silence.
- Consider a person's intentions as well as their words; not everyone is a skilled communicator.
- Be a good listener.

Competent communication is not simple; it is a set of skills that involve moderating your words and tone of voice. You must decide what to say and what not to say. This process involves good listening skills and a genuine effort to understand the other person, rather than an emphasis on "being heard." As you reminisce about your family dynamics, what role did communication play? Were there spoken or unspoken rules about how you communicated? As you think about your past experiences, what patterns of communication were modeled for you? What communication styles do you use with friends and family members? Do you notice a style of communication that works well for you, or are you aware of styles that interfere with your message?

Communication Barriers

A communication barrier blocks or inhibits the dynamic flow of communication. Barriers also can lead to a communication breakdown, resulting in a total failure in communication.

When I think of communication barriers within my family, the following comes to mind:

_____

_____

_____

When I think of communication breakdowns in my family, I think of:

_____

_____

_____

Do you have communication breakdowns you would like to repair? While in extreme cases, you may feel your differences are irreconcilable, in most situations by working on your communication techniques, you cannot only improve your skills, you also may be able to restore or strengthen important relationships. Effective communication is a skill set which may be learned, shared, and practiced every day.

Competent Communication

What it is:
- speaking clearly
- listening attentively
- engaging in dialogue
- honoring the relationship above being right
- knowing what not to say
- paying attention to vocal tone/ cues
- being aware of verbal and nonverbal gestures

What it is not:
- monopolizing the conversation
- interrupting others
- using offensive language
- having a communication breakdown

RECOGNIZING ROADBLOCKS

The inability to move beyond an impasse may compromise relationships, personal happiness, and may damage self-esteem. As previously mentioned, anger, hurt feelings, and misunderstandings are potential hazards that might create stumbling blocks for bereaved people coping with grief. As you progress on your journey, be aware of possible roadblocks where you or your loved ones may become bogged down, get stuck, or spiral downward. By recognizing potential barriers, or areas where you are currently stuck, you have the opportunity to develop practical solutions that will restore hope and help avoid future problems.

Internal Signals

Be on the lookout for these potential warning signs:

- Low self-esteem: may include self-critical thoughts or behaviors, overly-dependent attachments or relationships, lack of boundaries, inadequate self-care, identifying with a victim mentality

- Depletion: feeling drained physically, emotionally, financially, spiritually

- Unrealistic expectations: feeling the need to be the strong one, attempting to get over the loss too quickly, denial, setting high standards for others

- Loss of hope: depression, toxic feelings, social isolation, relentless regret, refusal to accept the loss, suicidal thoughts, self-destructive behaviors

External Triggers

- Special days: holidays, birthdays, anniversaries

- Complicated grief issues: bereavement overload,

addictions, attachment or avoidance issues

- Unmet expectations: feelings of abandonment or betrayal when others disappoint you, fail to meet your needs or do not provide support

- Interpersonal conflicts: intolerance of people, holding a grudge, anger, aberrant or mean-spirited behavior, communication breakdowns

Beyond Bumps and Barriers

How do people move beyond obstacles, get back on the road, and drive forward? Wounded grievers have shared that it is helpful to first acknowledge the signals. Often times, you know on some level when you are stuck, or trusted friends may have shared their concerns. By accepting that you may need to work on some issues, you are mentally preparing yourself to focus on moving past the block. Be open to asking for and accepting help when needed. Implement strategies for staying the course. You may find that you will be forced to deal with old problems that you now see in a new or magnified light, but honor your effort by acknowledging that it is worth the time and energy required. Being aware of warning signs, and the knowledge that others have successfully worked through volatile situations may be the combination you need to encourage and empower yourself and those you care about.

Grief challenges a person's self-esteem; status and self-identity may have shifted. A poor self-image prior to experiencing a loss does not magically improve when a death has occurred. And in fact it may become more challenged as the additional stress of grieving can shake even the most positive of self-images. Grieving is depleting and the process of reconciling our grief is demanding.

Specific days, people, or places may trigger a grief response that is both surprising and embarrassing. You may feel out of control or victimized by your own emotions. You may find that you feel overly attached to favorite possessions and mementos, are unable to part with anything that belonged to your loved one, or find that you cannot even look at or touch anything that belonged to the deceased.

Breaking Through

Many bereaved people say they believe that their deceased loved one would want them to cherish and enjoy life, and would not want them to mourn indefinitely. Just as it is important to give oneself permission to grieve, sometimes, it is necessary to give oneself permission to heal. Making a conscious decision to begin to release some of the pain of your grief may be necessary to move past current roadblocks. There are times when you may need to go deep within yourself to call upon your inner resources to give yourself the strength and courage to break out of a downward spiral. Depending upon your unique situation, the following strategies for moving past gridlock may be helpful.

Be your own advocate

- Establish and respect healthy boundaries. Do not be shy about asking for what you need or saying no when appropriate.

- Engage in healthy practices. Eat and sleep in accordance with your own needs. Exercise regularly.

- Stay connected with friends and family.

- Participate in social events on your terms – make arrangements that are comfortable for you; if necessary, drive your own car, meet people at the event, limit the time you will be there, etc.

- Make plans, but be flexible – if you are not up to going on the day of the event, give yourself permission to take a pass or schedule another date.

- Do not isolate yourself – sometimes, turn off the television or computer and challenge yourself to go out. Try to spend time with others.

Challenge yourself

- Create new rituals to mark special occasions.

- Declutter – when you are ready, start parting with the things that you no longer need, even if they belonged to your loved one. If you find it difficult, but are sure you are ready, focus on the benefit others will receive.

- Replace negative or critical messages with positive self-talk. Celebrate your achievements, no matter how small.

- Do things you are able to do for yourself. It will build your confidence and enthusiasm.

Be patient

- Progress may be slow at first and setbacks may occur. Persevere.

- Get a buddy. Make arrangements with a trusted friend to support each other through "down days."

Relax, reflect, and recharge each day.

-Meghan Yudes

_____

_____

_____

_____

_____

_____

_____

_____

_____

_____

_____

_____

_____

_____

_____

_____

_____

_____

_____

_____

_____

_____

At the time of your loss, take time to grieve. Society urges us to get back to normal as quickly as possible. Don't rush your grief. Our jobs gave us "three days" to grieve and we were expected to be productive. I found three years wasn't enough.

-N.Z.

Mother whose son completed suicide

_____

_____

_____

_____

_____

_____

_____

_____

_____

_____

_____

_____

_____

_____

_____

_____

_____

_____

_____

_____

_____

_____

_____

Blessed are those who mourn for they shall be comforted.

-Matthew 5:4

Keep your heart open for as long as you can, as wide as you can, for others and especially yourself.
-Morrie Schwartz

_____

_____

_____

_____

_____

_____

_____

_____

_____

_____

_____

_____

_____

_____

_____

_____

_____

_____

_____

_____

_____

_____

Key Insights

What have I learned about myself?

_____

_____

_____

What have I learned about my
relationship with others?

_____

_____

_____

What have I learned about my loss?

_____

_____

_____

What have I learned about my grief?

_____

_____

_____

Chapter Four: Rest Stop

As many who have gone through the grief process will testify, grieving can be an exhausting experience. At times, one may feel physically, emotionally, and mentally depleted. Experts in the field tell us that this sense of depletion is both common and valuable, as one of the functions of grieving is to force us to slow down, to turn inward, and to give us time to face all of our feelings related to the loss. Eventually as grieving people grow stronger, they learn to restructure their lives, to rebuild and renew. The goal is not to forget our losses, but rather to integrate them into our lives, and to go on living.

Yet what does one do while waiting for that healing to occur? How do bereaved people cope each day, even on those days when they may question if they have the strength to function, to care for their families, to go to work, to meet their obligations, and to carry on with their daily activities? One answer rests in learning how to consistently practice self-care. As part of your grief journey, you have the opportunity to discover what you really need to take care of yourself. Use this time to calm your spirit, soothe your soul, and reenergize your body. As you slow down, and give yourself the freedom to rest, you may find yourself opening up to new experiences and reconnecting with forgotten or never-realized passions. Perhaps you used to enjoy drawing, fishing, writing, playing a musical instrument, or participating in a sport. Maybe you have longed to read all of the great American novels, take a cooking class, or learn a new hobby. Now may be the time to pursue those interests, or discover new passions. Find something that captures your imagination and give yourself permission to take a chance on trying something new. Do not feel that you have to be the best, just try to enjoy the experience. You may find that you discover not only new outlets for your creativity, but the opportunity to develop new friendships as well.

How to get started

If you are feeling physically and emotionally drained, you may feel it is easier to just stay where you are than to open yourself up to new experiences. Keep in mind that one of the best ways to reestablish a sense of balance in your life, is to be open to new challenges. It may take some work on your part, and it may require a commitment to try something new. But you can do it, if you break it down into small manageable steps, pay attention to your physical and emotional needs, and take it one step at a time. Start by reevaluating your priorities. Is it difficult for you to put yourself first? Do you make time for yourself to pursue your own interests? Do you prioritize time spent with people who nurture and uplift you?

Make yourself a priority

Do you know what renews your mind, body, and spirit? If you have a sense of those activities you would like to use to revitalize your energy, write them down. Set specific goals to bring them into your life. If you are not sure what would refresh your mind and body, use the exercises in this chapter to help get a sense of what you long for, to reconnect with favorite activities you may have given up along the way, or to develop new ones. As you work through the exercises, you may find it necessary to give yourself permission to take a "grief break." Think of this time as a rest stop on your grief journey. Use it to celebrate what remains in your life. Focus on your strengths. Learn how to replenish yourself so that when you must face the continued challenges of your grief, you will do so with renewed strength and vitality.

Today I am living life more fully and completely. I think more about how I want to spend the rest of my life. Time is not infinite.

-S.N.
Aunt whose nephew died in a car accident

Learning what's going on inside you can be difficult, but it's also invigorating, and the rewards are enormous.

-Barbara Sher

Self-Care Inventory

Self-care begins with positive, nurturing self-talk. It is being kind to yourself and considerate of your own needs and priorities. This initial step may be challenging, particularly if you have accepted the myth that being kind and generous to yourself, and making your own needs a priority, is something negative or selfish. Implementing a program of self-care may feel uncomfortable, at first, especially if you are used to putting your own needs last. However, give it a try. Give yourself permission to say no to some things (and some people) so that you can say yes to others. Do the things that you want to do, instead of only the things you think you ought to do. Spend time in the company of people who fill you up, motivate and inspire you. Allow yourself to laugh again. Focus on nutrition, exercise, and restoring a sense of balance to your life.

Take a few minutes to think about the things you can do to bring balance into your life. Check the activities you enjoy.

Things I enjoy doing:

- ☐ gardening
- ☐ golfing/fishing/outdoor activities
- ☐ exercising/playing sports
- ☐ writing a letter
- ☐ watching a movie or sporting event
- ☐ attending a concert or play
- ☐ reading a book
- ☐ cooking/trying a new recipe
- ☐ sharing a meal with a friend
- ☐ taking a drive/bicycling
- ☐ using the computer/spending time online
- ☐ taking a soothing bath
- ☐ getting a manicure, massage, or visiting a spa
- ☐ buying yourself or others a gift
- ☐ singing, playing, or listening to music

- ☐ dancing
- ☐ scrapbooking/ woodworking/ crafting
- ☐ doing random acts of kindness /volunteering
- ☐ organizing family photographs /family history
- ☐ spending time in nature
- ☐ visiting with children/grandchildren
- ☐ traveling

- ☐ other:_____

Things I used to enjoy, but have not had time for lately:

_____

_____

_____

Things I've never done but would like to try:

_____

_____

_____

Small steps I can take to move toward self-care today:

_____

_____

_____

Several of my girlfriends took me to a spa for a massage. That was amazing and unexpectedly pampering. One friend keeps me regularly in cards and chocolates.

-P.B.
Sister who is grieving the loss of her brother

_____

_____

_____

_____

_____

_____

_____

_____

_____

_____

_____

_____

_____

_____

_____

_____

_____

_____

_____

_____

_____

_____

_____

Learning to live in the present moment is part of the path of joy.

-Sarah Ban Breathnach

R Factor: Relationship to Self

Our longest and most important relationship is the one with self. Just as with every other aspect of life, how one copes with grief is often heavily influenced by one's commitment to self-care, one's internal dialogue (self-talk) and one's sense of self (self-esteem). If a person, particularly a grieving person, does not place a high priority on self, his or her health may be compromised, relationships may suffer, and ultimately the quality of life may be diminished.

There is a powerful connection between our attitude about self-care and our self-image. It is vital that a person recognizes the link between caring for one's self, that is prioritizing one's own physical and emotional needs, and feeling worthy of the effort. If you are used to putting everyone's needs above your own, you may not see the value in taking proper care of yourself. However, our physical strength and health is not inexhaustible, and if it is not guarded carefully, it can become depleted to the point of physical illness or emotional exhaustion.

Self-care involves getting proper nutrition, sleep, and exercise. It also involves nurturing relationships that are important to our well-being and seeking balance in our lives. When our priorities are in sync with self-care, our self-talk becomes more positive. It is easier to choose positive messages and affirmations, and filter out negative ones, as our emotional resiliency is fueled by our physical sense of well-being. Our self-esteem is also raised as it is easier to feel good about ourselves, and easier to love and accept ourselves.

Celebrate your accomplishments

When you think of your own self-image, what comes to mind? Do you automatically think of your unique gifts and talents? Does a list of your accomplishments flash into your mind? Do you routinely take the time to self-assess your own abilities and accomplishments? Take time, right now, to appreciate yourself for who you are, as well as what you have accomplished. Be aware of how others perceive you. Ask trusted friends or family members for feedback if you are uncertain. How strong is your self-image? If you overheard a negative comment about yourself, would you accept it without question, or dismiss it without consideration? What if the comment you overheard was positive, would you find it more or less difficult to accept?

Live an authentic life

When you hear the term "leading an authentic life," what does that mean to you? For some, it means being true to oneself, honoring that inner voice that resonates within your core being. Are you able to be yourself with others? Are you able to express your unique views and share your individual talents? Being yourself with others may not always be easy; sometimes there may be trade-offs in following your true path. You may be called upon to make sacrifices; however, in order to live your life with meaning and purpose, you may have to make difficult choices at times. Hold fast to your values, and stay true to your inner wisdom, and an authentic life will be your reward.

Sit down, take out your favorite stationery, and write yourself a love letter. Tell yourself why you are such a special person, what your unique gifts are, and why you enjoy being – you. Mail it to yourself and when you receive it, read it over and add any new thoughts. Put your love letter in a special place where you can easily access it whenever you need a special boost of self-confidence or a reminder of your self-worth.

Our primary relationship is really with ourselves. Our relationships with other people constantly reflect exactly where we are in the process.

-Shakti Gawain

_____

_____

_____

_____

_____

_____

_____

_____

_____

_____

_____

_____

_____

_____

_____

_____

_____

_____

_____

_____

_____

_____

 *I am considerably more aware of my place in the universe and the value of time. As a result, I am determined to be more conscious of how I use my time, and with whom I spend my time.*

-D.G.

Self-Talk

Self-talk is the inner voice that communicates messages to us. It is estimated that a person has between 50,000 - 80,000 thoughts a day. Think of the impact it would have if only half of the things you thought about yourself were critical or negative. So guard your thoughts and self-talk carefully. If you make a negative comment about yourself, or become aware of a critical thought, stop and replace it immediately with a positive one. Watch your language too as often what is spoken gives more energy to fleeting thoughts. Look for the positive. If you are feeling down, try to shift your thoughts to something you are looking forward to, tell yourself that tomorrow will be a better day, or look for a positive side to your feelings. Take time to notice and celebrate your accomplishments, no matter how small, and start developing a "happiness habit." Just as what you tell yourself can lead to a negative self-image, filling your mind and heart with positive self-talk can lead to a happier and more optimistic outlook.

Whether the messages you tell yourself are the result of your own beliefs or have been internalized from others' comments, they are subject to change. Although they often occur automatically, like instant messages, by making yourself consciously aware of their content, you can change their impact. And as you continue to work on reframing negative messages, you probably will find that your self-talk becomes more positive as well.

Self-talk tips

- Be aware of your own internal dialogue
- Focus on positive messages and thoughts
- Use self-talk to encourage growth/change
- Stop and replace negative messages with positive ones
- Acknowledge progress; celebrate improvements

_____

_____

_____

_____

_____

_____

_____

_____

_____

_____

_____

_____

_____

_____

_____

_____

_____

_____

_____

_____

_____

_____

_____

Enjoy the little things, for one day you may look back and realize they were the big things.

-Robert Brault

Self-Esteem

Who do you see when you look in your mirror? Do you like the person you have become? Can you celebrate your achievements? Take pride in your relationships with your family and friends? Or do you tend to focus on what you do not like about yourself? Do you remember your failures more easily than your successes?

Our initial sense of self comes from our early relationships with family members, friends, teachers and peers. Through our interactions with them, our first impressions and opinions of ourselves are formed. The messages, feedback, judgments, criticisms, and praise received in these early encounters help to shape and define our self-image, our self-acceptance, and our self-worth. Our self-esteem affects every aspect of our lives. It impacts our relationships, and influences our vision of the world around us.

Why is self-esteem important?

Self-esteem may be defined as confidence and satisfaction in oneself. It relates to the regard or opinion one holds for oneself, whether it is positive or negative. While a person with too much self-esteem might be considered arrogant, generally, a high level of self-esteem is a healthy, positive, and desirable characteristic. Healthy self-esteem enables you to feel good about yourself and your relationships. Others also tend to enjoy being with people with a positive self-image.

On the other hand, having low self-esteem is often associated with depression, oppression, and conflicted or failed relationships. People with a poor self-image may be more self-conscious, less aware of the needs of others, and seek frequent reassurance which often may strain relationships. In the extreme, low self-esteem may even turn deadly in that a person with very low self-esteem may feel as if his or her life is hopeless or worthless and may become suicidal.

How would you rate yourself in terms of your self-esteem? Has your self-image been altered by your loss? Do you need to build up your self-esteem?

How to build self-esteem

Increasing your self-esteem is both a simple and difficult task. It is simple in that it merely requires you to change your opinion of yourself. It is difficult in that you may bump up against some long-held beliefs. For instance, if you "always" thought of yourself as a fearful or dependent person, how do you now step out of the shadows? Or if you felt you have "always" had to be the strong one in the family, how do you now ask for help? The short answer is the same one you need to approach any new task or endeavor — you can do it if you break it down and take it one step at a time.

Here are some tips that you may find helpful.

- Surround yourself with positive support. Share your desire to build up your confidence and ask those closest to you to remind you of your accomplishments.

- Try new things and celebrate your successes. You will never know what you might have a talent or gift for unless you try.

- Do things you love. Enthusiasm is contagious and when you follow your bliss, good things will happen.

- Help others. Volunteer your time in a local shelter, hospital, school, club, or organization. It's a great way to feel good about yourself while helping others.

- Accept yourself and give yourself permission to grow.

My greatest comforts were those friends and family who allowed me to feel a full range of emotions as many times as necessary to work through the pain. I needed to cry, to scream, to feel guilty, to feel ashamed, to be angry with God, to curse my religion and find it again, and finally to let myself be loved — in spite of my shattered self-esteem.

-N.Z.

_____

_____

_____

_____

_____

_____

_____

_____

_____

_____

_____

_____

_____

_____

_____

_____

_____

_____

_____

_____

_____

Self-esteem is so delicate a flower that praise tends to make it bloom, while discouragement often nips it in the bud.

-Alex F. Osborn

REFUELING

While your loss may have left you feeling empty or less secure in the world, you have the inner resources to refuel. Just for now, try looking through another lens. Oftentimes, people do not value self-care or celebrate their accomplishments. However, by changing focus and reframing attitudes and behaviors, one can learn to acknowledge one's own accomplishments, recognize individual talents, and celebrate personal strengths.

By answering the following questions, you may gain a new perspective on your own strengths and accomplishments.

With whom would you like to spend more time?

_____

_____

_____

Describe an ideal day. Provide specific details as you visualize this experience.

_____

_____

_____

What fulfills and energizes you?

_____

_____

_____

What do you feel is your greatest accomplishment?

_____

_____

_____

What brings you joy?

_____

_____

_____

Describe an activity that relaxes and renews you.

_____

_____

_____

List three things that you will commit to doing in order to refuel your mind and body.

_____

_____

_____

Tip: Sometimes a quiet retreat may be hard to find. If you do not have an area in your home where you can get away to refuel, look for creative options. Sometimes a corner of a room, or a shelf decorated with personal mementos, or a few minutes outdoors, can lift your spirit.

Just for fun...

Take an old deck of playing cards or fifty-two pieces of paper. On each card, write one nice thing that you would enjoy doing. (Examples: attend an athletic event, take a warm bubble bath, buy a special book, enjoy an ice cream cone, have lunch with a friend, get a massage, buy yourself flowers, see a movie, etc.) Put the cards away. Pull one out and do whatever the card says whenever you feel the need for a little relaxation, pampering, or joy in your life.

Or...

Create a pamper basket

If you were asked to create a basket of items that would relax your body, ease your mind, and soothe your spirit, what would you select? Draw a basket or box and fill it with your favorite things. If you aren't feeling that creative right now, simply list the items below.

_____

_____

_____

_____

_____

_____

_____

_____

_____

Griefstruck

My friend, Karen, supported her mother through a tough battle with cancer. Karen called to let me know that her mother was nearing death. She asked me, as the funeral director, what personal items would be needed when the time came for a visitation/wake. In reviewing the checklist, I mentioned nylons, socks or pantyhose. Karen replied: "I do not think anyone should spend eternity in pantyhose." We both laughed through our tears, grateful for a moment of relief during this difficult time.

-M.O'C.

Checkpoint

How do you see yourself now? How healthy is your self-image?

_____

_____

How would you like to see yourself?

_____

_____

Think about how you take care of yourself. How well do you balance self-care, family, and work responsibilities? Do you place a high value on taking care of yourself?

_____

_____

What would help build your self-esteem? How can you move toward accomplishing that goal?

_____

_____

What volunteer activity do you think you would enjoy? How can you get started?

_____

_____

Learn to get in touch with the silence within yourself and know that everything in this life has a purpose.
-Dr. Elisabeth Kubler-Ross

_____

_____

_____

_____

_____

_____

_____

_____

_____

_____

_____

_____

_____

_____

_____

_____

_____

_____

_____

_____

_____

_____

What lies behind us and what lies before us are tiny matters, compared to what lies within us.
-Ralph Waldo Emerson

I attended the visitation of a friend's brother, who died suddenly and unexpectedly. As part of a large family, the siblings lightheartedly had come to use their chronological birth order as nicknames. At the wake, each sibling and all of their family members wore name tags which identified their name, relationship, and "number". It was heartwarming to see their sense of connection displayed in this creative manner.

-M.O'C.

Humor and Grief

One of the changes bereaved people often notice about their lives is that the joy just seems to have been drained out of it. It is not unusual to hear grieving people share that they cannot remember the last time they laughed or found anything even mildly amusing. However, this is not the case for everyone, even for some who have experienced a recent loss. What makes the difference?

Many factors affect our sense of humor – everything from our individual personality to our culture to our specific life circumstances. If you find that it is difficult to share a laugh with a friend, or if you have been offended by someone's inappropriate use of humor during your time of grieving, take a moment to look closer at the situation. What would sharing a moment of joy again mean to you? Would you feel guilty if you told a joke or laughed at a funny incident? Do you think that laughing is disrespectful or a sign that you or others have forgotten, or moved past, the pain of your loss?

For many, humor is a coping mechanism. Laughter, like tears, can provide a release for pent-up emotion. Sometimes people may make light-hearted comments, which may seem inappropriate, as a way of dealing with the stress they are feeling. For others, humor simply has become a natural release valve – a way to help cope with daily challenges. For everyone, laughter can be healing. Sharing a belly laugh can stimulate our biochemistry and produce endorphins which can lift our mood, ease physical pain, and produce a sense of well-being. Laughter can help discharge negative emotions like anger or rage as well as help us ease the effects of stress. So if laughter is returning to your life, welcome it; and if it never left, consider yourself fortunate.

He who laughs, lasts.

-Mary Pettibone Poole

What makes you laugh?

Since laughter is therapeutic to both your body and spirit, it is a good idea to pay attention to what makes you laugh. As you find a funny cartoon or humorous story in a magazine or newspaper, cut it out and post it on your refrigerator or bulletin board. Keep your eyes and ears open for light-hearted stories or funny things your children, grandchildren, nieces, or nephews say or do. Write them down in a notebook or start a file folder and create your own "laughalogue." Add cartoons, funny quotes, and jokes as you come across them. Soon you will have a resource you may go to whenever you need a laugh or would like to share a funny story with a friend.

Be on the lookout for things that make you smile.

Take the time to surround yourself with things that bring a little joy into your life. Some days a single flower may be all you need; other days you may want to break out a rhinestone tiara, a clown nose, funny glasses, a silly hat or laminated button. Keep a stash of inexpensive toys such as yo-yos, paper airplanes, finger puppets, jacks, a box of crayons, anything that catches your eye and looks fun, in a special box or drawer. When you need a lift, spend some time indulging your inner child - and you may find you "both" have a good laugh.

Share your good times with a friend.

One of the best ways to lift your spirits is to reach out to a friend. Call or email someone who never fails to make you laugh or someone who you think may need a smile, too. Share one of your jokes or funny stories, and you'll both feel better. Or invite a friend over and rent a funny movie, watch reruns of your favorite television show or play a child's card game like "Crazy Eights." A good laugh is a great way to refresh your mind, body, and spirit.

Tip: Check out your local library or bookstore for humorous books. Also bookmark your favorite websites for daily jokes.

Laughter is the closest distance between two people.

-Victor Borge

_____

_____

_____

_____

_____

_____

_____

_____

_____

_____

_____

_____

_____

_____

_____

_____

_____

_____

_____

_____

_____

_____

_____

_____

_____

_____

_____

_____

_____

_____

_____

_____

_____

_____

_____

_____

_____

_____

_____

_____

_____

_____

_____

_____

My husband and I try to keep focused by looking for the 'small miracles' every day. We listen for the cardinal's song, a message from a friend, the sight of a rainbow, sunrise, sunset, and transform this hope one step at a time. We developed a new perspective that accepts that we are different.

-N. Z.
Bereaved Mother

If you could write yourself a prescription for self-care, what would it be? Would you focus on taking better care of yourself, improving your internal dialogue, or building your self-esteem?

Write a prescription to address your area of greatest need.

R_x For Self-Care

Name: _____

Date: __/__/__

Fill By: __/__/__

Refills: _unlimited_

Key Insights

What have I learned about myself?

_____

_____

_____

What have I learned about my
relationship with others?

_____

_____

_____

What have I learned about my loss?

_____

_____

_____

What have I learned about my grief?

_____

_____

_____

Chapter Five: Changing Lanes

Experiencing a loss may trigger a series of physical, emotional and spiritual changes in one's life. Some grief counselors suggest that grieving people should not make any major life changes within the first year following a significant loss. However, that may not always be possible, practical, or in their best interest. In some cases, bereaved family members have had to leave their home, give up a familiar job, change schools, take on new work responsibilities, or relocate to a new area while in the midst of their own grieving. Death is considered a primary loss, but it often brings about secondary losses as well. The impact of these secondary losses should be acknowledged. For example, bereaved people often find themselves in a position of trying to adjust to lifestyle changes while grieving the loss of a loved one. While such changes are the reality of our world, they may stretch one's coping skills, almost to the breaking point.

Our ability to cope with primary and secondary losses also may be influenced by the nature of the loss. For example, when people have experienced a sudden or traumatic loss, it is not unusual for them to be left feeling shaken, alone, and vulnerable. In other situations, where the death was more expected, people have reported feeling better prepared to cope with the loss, despite their pain and sorrow. Some grieving people feel a sense of acceptance, a quiet resignation, especially in situations where they may feel the person either had lost the quality of his or her life, or had enjoyed a full and rewarding life. In these instances, family members often describe a sense of peaceful acceptance, although they still grieve the loss of their loved one.

The death of a loved one is an unwanted change. It is difficult to prepare for all of the challenges and transitions that often accompany loss, and yet, for many people loss is also a transformative experience. It holds the potential to change a person in a positive way, as eventually one learns to adapt and comes to feel that he or she has grown as a result of the experience and its "life lessons." Loss also may help us feel a deeper, soulful connection with God, nature, and each other. Grief can open our hearts and minds to new possibilities. The death of a loved one may point a person in a new direction. A significant loss may cause one to choose a new career, take on new responsibilities, reorder priorities, or make other major life changes.

Just as you may choose to change lanes while driving down a highway, to slow down or speed up, to avoid a hazardous situation or adjust to traveling conditions, from time to time, you may need to change lanes on your grief journey as well. As you confront your loss, and face your own mortality (perhaps for the first time), you can easily feel disoriented . . . overwhelmed . . . confused or lost. You may question what you thought you knew, challenge core beliefs and relationships, and fear your ability to cope with what lies ahead. You may feel abandoned, insecure, and uncertain. It is important to remember that even during this time of uncertainty, you still are in the driver's seat. You hold the key to establishing boundaries, and even to choosing another road, if that is what you decide. You can slow down when you need to, go faster when you are feeling strong, and get off the road (take a grief break) any time you feel the need to relax, renew and refuel.

At 4:30 each day, I was still expecting him to come home. I would look for his red truck. It was a hard time of day for me, and I found it helped to change my routine. Now I try to fill up that time. I will eat an early dinner, take a walk or try to do something outdoors.

-R. T.
Wife whose husband died 10 weeks ago

Priorities are destined to change. We needed to decide now: What is life really about? Things that once seemed important aren't any more. We found life is not about how much money you make, your title, your educational degree, the car your drive, or who you know. Our challenge was to accept that life is not about what happened to us — but rather about how we responded to our loss.

-N.Z.

_____

_____

_____

_____

_____

_____

_____

_____

_____

_____

_____

_____

_____

_____

_____

_____

_____

_____

_____

_____

_____

_____

Continuity gives us roots; change gives us branches, letting us stretch and grow and reach new heights.
-Pauline R. Kezer

Life can only be understood backwards, but it must be lived forward.

-Soren Kierkegaard

R Factor: Relationship to Change

Change happens with or without our consent. You may feel that change has been thrust upon you. How one copes with change directly affects the outcome of a situation, and can influence our happiness or sadness. Change is a part of life and a part of loss. The world would be a less exciting place if people, places, things, and relationships stayed the same. So why do so many of us fear or resist change?

- Change may be uncomfortable. Choosing not to change keeps us in our comfort zone. Oftentimes, a person chooses the familiar until discomfort propels us to change.

- Change requires effort. Choosing not to change is often easier, even though there are consequences.

- Change requires us to let go of the past. Sometimes resisting change is an attempt to keep things as they have always been, to allow us to hold on to what a person has always thought, felt, or done, and to avoid moving into an unknown or uncertain future.

How would you describe your relationship to change? Do you tolerate it, accept it, welcome it as an exciting challenge, or do you fear it, resist it, or dread it as an uncomfortable but inevitable part of life? Has your relationship with change altered over the course of your life? It may be new to you to think of having a relationship with change and yet change is a part of our life from birth. As you grow, you change. As you learn, you change. As you mature, you change. As you fall in love, experience accomplishment or disappointment, buy a car or home, start a relationship, commit to a family, face challenges, succeed, fail, and experience life, you change.

Resisting change takes energy and can sabotage your happiness and success. However, for many of us, accepting change is a process which occurs over time. People often change one thought or one action at a time. Gradually, one can learn to not only accept, but to actually welcome, direct, and celebrate change.

The positive side of change

It is not unusual to think of change as negative. As often one is unable to control the changes that occur in one's life, it is natural to fear change. However without change, growth could not take place. As you look back on the changes that have happened in your life since you experienced your loss, have they been positive, negative, or a combination of both? For a few minutes, focus on the positive changes that have taken place since your loss. You may have to work a little to find the up side of the changes but most changes do come with an opportunity if you look at them from a positive perspective. For instance, having to handle all of the financial matters for the first time may provide you with a new skill set and increased self-reliance. Having to move to a new home may provide you with an opportunity for a fresh start, a chance to declutter, and make new friends. Give it a try. You may be surprised how many positive changes you may find once you start looking for them.

I have learned that life can be capricious and that despite what we think, we have very little control over the events that occur in our lives. However, I do have control over my response to those events. I chose to respond with dignity and grace.

-P.B.

Changing Gears

Take time to reflect on and journal about your answers to the following questions. Remember there are no right or wrong answers, just information to be gained, and perhaps valuable insights into your own thoughts and attitudes toward change.

How do you feel about change?

_____

_____

_____

What did your family model for you about change?

_____

_____

_____

What messages did you internalize about change?

_____

_____

_____

How well do you adapt to change?

_____

_____

_____

How do you wish you reacted to change?

_____

_____

_____

What steps could you take to make your wish a reality?

_____

_____

_____

What major life changes have you experienced and how have they influenced your attitude toward change?

_____

_____

_____

Choose to take control. Allowing your past hurt to control you can paralyze what you do in the future.

-N.Z.

Losing the only parent you've ever known has a profound negative impact. The sadness and sense of irretrievable loss are intense, but so is the determination to stay close to my siblings. I am considering moving back to the Midwest.

-K.O'C.
Daughter whose mother died 13 months ago

There are some things you learn best in calm, and some in storm.

-Willa Cather

Checkpoint

The death of someone you loved is a life-altering event. Your life will never be the same. Yet how it has changed, and how it will continue to change, will vary based on a number of factors. While you will not ever "get over" the death, you have the opportunity to reconcile the loss, to incorporate lessons learned, and to discover new strengths and abilities. This checklist is designed to help you identify how your loss has changed your life. This exercise will also help you prepare for the changes yet to come.

How have you been changed by loss ?

Physically, have you experienced...

- ☐ Changes in your overall health and body
- ☐ Changes in your physical appearance
- ☐ Changes in your daily routine or habits
- ☐ Changes in your living arrangements or residence

Financially, have you noticed...

- ☐ An increase, decrease or no change in status
- ☐ That you have assumed new financial responsibilities
- ☐ That your savings or income has been affected
- ☐ Increased or decreased financial concerns

Socially, are you aware of...

- ☐ A changed social status
- ☐ Formation of new or loss of old friendships

- [ ] Being closer to or more distant from family members
- [ ] Having a support system and community resources

Spiritually, have you experienced...

- [ ] A changed relationship with God
- [ ] Altered religious beliefs
- [ ] Changed attendance at religious services
- [ ] New beliefs regarding an afterlife
- [ ] A difference in spiritual support

Emotionally, have you felt...

- [ ] Greater ease or difficulty in expressing your feelings
- [ ] More compassion or empathy with others
- [ ] A different attitude toward companionship
- [ ] Changes in intimacy
- [ ] An increase or decrease in stress
- [ ] More or less connected with others
- [ ] More extreme emotions or mood swings

Personally, have you identified...

- [ ] Changes in your self-identity
- [ ] An altered sense of safety and security
- [ ] Practical coping skills
- [ ] What stresses or relaxes you
- [ ] Increased or decreased self-worth

What three things would you **not** want to change about your life now?

_____

_____

_____

Sail Away

Imagine you are about to embark on a trip to a desert island. All of your physical needs (food, water, clothes, shelter) will be taken care of; however you have to bring whatever else is necessary to satisfy your other needs.

What would you bring?

1. _____

2. _____

3. _____

4. _____

5. _____

6. _____

7. _____

8. _____

9. _____

10. _____

Now take a look at your list of essential items. What does it tell you about what you value? As you review your list, do you see a pattern? Circle the numbers of your top three priorities.

_____

_____

_____

_____

_____

_____

_____

_____

_____

_____

_____

_____

_____

_____

_____

_____

_____

_____

_____

_____

_____

_____

Tomorrow is the most important thing in life. Comes into us at midnight very clean. It's perfect when it arrives and it puts itself in our hands. It hopes we've learned something from yesterday.

-John Wayne

Never fear shadows. They simply mean there's a light shining somewhere nearby.

–Ruth Renkel

It hurts to "let go." Letting go is the conscious act of choosing freedom over self-punishment. We couldn't change what had happened. We had to face the fact that the past was over.

-N.Z.

Mother whose son completed suicide

New Directions

In times of crisis and confusion, you may find the familiar – comforting. Doing things the way you have always done them can help get you through the difficult days when making even the smallest decision may seem overwhelming. However, repeating the same actions, and holding on to the same thoughts and feelings also can keep you from experiencing new opportunities and developing new skills.

The goal of this exercise is to encourage you to expand your horizons, to do, think, or feel things differently. It is important when you are approaching this task however that you set realistic objectives. Be mindful of how recently you experienced your loss and where you are in your grief journey. Be gentle with yourself. If you are still at a stage when you are experiencing feelings of disorganization and confusion, if what used to be a simple decision still feels challenging, then start with something small. For example, if you usually drive the same way to work, to the store, or to a place of worship, try a new route, and be aware of your changed surroundings. If you feel ready to take on a challenge, set a more aggressive goal.

If you are uncertain what behaviors or thoughts you would like to change, review the exercises in Chapter Four for ideas. Try something that you have always wanted to do. Consider trying a new hobby or a new activity, take a class in something that interests you, plan a weekend trip - do something just for you. Celebrate your success, no matter how small, and incorporate your new experiences into your daily routine. Once you have successfully expanded your tolerance for small changes, you may feel ready to move on to more significant challenges.

Here is my plan for something new and different:

_____

_____

_____

I did it!   Describe what you did differently and how it felt.

_____

_____

_____

Next step... here's how I am going to incorporate my new skills or ideas into my daily routine.

_____

_____

_____

Moving on... the next challenge I want to work on is:

_____

_____

_____

My first step toward achieving my new goal will be:

_____

_____

_____

I will complete that step by:

_____

_____

The journey of a thousand miles begins with one step.

-Lao Tzu

Griefstruck

Sometimes our grief journey can bless us with a unique perspective. A gentleman shared with me that his daughter had told him that she felt it was time to start putting away some of the photographs of his late wife, especially the one he kept by his bedside. It showed his wife, near the end of her battle with cancer, with her balding head wrapped in a scarf. His daughter thought her mother looked pale and sick, and found the picture to be a painful reminder of her death. The gentleman disagreed and felt his daughter wasn't really seeing the picture. When he looked at it all he saw was the beautiful smile on his wife's face and the sparkle in her eye because she was looking at their youngest grandchild. The picture reminded him of a wonderful afternoon they all shared together, and brought him great comfort.

- M.A.G.

Change... Change... Change...

Not all of the changes in our lives are big or life-altering. However, sometimes even small changes can result in a new perspective or give us a new way of looking at our lives.

Read over the following list of small changes you could make in your life. Check off four changes you would be willing to try. Try one change, each week, for the next four weeks. Record any positive or negative reactions you have to each change.

- ☐ Order a new dish at your favorite restaurant.
- ☐ Wear a piece of clothing or color you would never have thought was your style.
- ☐ Find a new route to work.
- ☐ Listen to a new radio station.
- ☐ Get up 15 minutes earlier or go to bed 30 minutes later.
- ☐ Wear your watch on the opposite wrist.
- ☐ Buy a silly pair of socks – wear them all day.
- ☐ Eat at a new restaurant.
- ☐ Buy a new belt, tie or lipstick.
- ☐ Try a new recipe.
- ☐ Rearrange the furniture in your favorite room.
- ☐ Visit a museum.
- ☐ Have a cup of coffee with a new acquaintance.
- ☐ Eat lunch at a new time – earlier or later than usual.

Remember happiness doesn't depend upon who you are or what you have; it depends solely upon what you think.

-Dale Carnegie

It's amazing how quickly we return to our regular lives. I find myself distracted and forgetful. I have to continuously remind people that my brother died a short time ago. I'm not 'normal' yet. Sometimes, it feels like I'm using his death as an excuse, but I know that the changes in me are valid.

-P.B.
On the recent loss of her brother

THREE WISHES

When you have experienced a life-altering loss, your most sincere wish might be to somehow 'get back' the life you had before the death of your loved one. However, part of your grief work is to learn how to be in the world without your loved one by your side. It may be helpful to look at what you wish for yourself, beyond wanting your loved one to return.

If you could be granted any three wishes, what would you most desire? A wish may be as direct as to feel safe and secure again, or as practical as to be free from financial burdens and concerns.

My three wishes would be:

One:

_____

_____

_____

Two:

_____

_____

_____

Three:

_____

_____

_____

_____

_____

_____

_____

_____

_____

_____

_____

_____

_____

_____

_____

_____

_____

_____

_____

_____

_____

_____

_____

_____

 *Today when I recall it (father's suicide), I am filled with compassion for myself, my family, and by extension for all who have come face-to-face-with personal tragedies.*

-H.G.

When there is no going back...

Bereaved people have shared with us that once you have been griefstruck, you are forever changed. There is no going back. You have a changed perspective and an acquired wisdom. This change which often affects every aspect of one's life is so powerful that in spite of the pain, many grievers would not choose to go back to their former selves, if given the opportunity. So, what is different for you now? What changes have your loss brought into your life that you now know resonate within your very essence? Certainly, you have accumulated more resources and skills in coping with change than you may realize – and perhaps even more than you ever thought possible. But is there something more? Think about how you have adapted to your loss so far – how has your view of life and death changed?

The changes that are brought about by the death of someone you loved affect every aspect of your life. Grieving people often describe themselves as being changed from the inside, out. They may feel more open, vulnerable, grateful, compassionate, enlightened, and insightful. It is as if there was a blow to their equilibrium, everything shifted, and when things finally were put back together, they all were in a different place. Priorities were drastically changed. In addition to countless personal changes, many of those whose lives have been touched by loss have helped others in their family, their friends, and in some cases, even reached out to their community by creating charitable foundations, support groups, community programs, publications, organizations, bereavement ministries, or working to support relevant legislation.

What will your legacy of change be? Nurture the seeds of change which have been planted within your own heart – and amazing things may happen for you, for your family, and for your community.

It is never too late to be what you might have been.
-George Eliot

Key Insights

What have I learned about myself?

_____

_____

_____

What have I learned about my
relationship with others?

_____

_____

_____

What have I learned about my loss?

_____

_____

_____

What have I learned about my grief?

_____

_____

_____

Chapter Six: Traveling Conditions

You experience many different conditions as you travel through life. Sometimes the road is smooth; sometimes, it is full of bumps, potholes, hills, valleys and detours. Like any road trip, life may present challenges. While it is difficult to anticipate what lies ahead for each of us, some of our most cherished moments often grow out of difficult life challenges. And as challenges are met and overcome, lessons about loyalty, friendship, faith and courage are learned.

As you navigate your way through life's unexpected or unfamiliar roads, you may be forced to slow down. And so it is with your grief journey as well. You may find that you are forced to slow down, to turn your focus inward, and try to gain a better understanding of who you are, what you have lost, and what you value most.

Your grief journey often turns your focus outward too, as it may cause you to think about who you enjoy spending time with and who helps comfort you when you need comforting most. You may want one person to fill all of your needs, but that is probably not possible. Family and friends are invaluable in that they give you the opportunity to love and be loved, to provide support and to be supported. According to Adina Wrobleski, a bereaved parent and author, "One of the biggest lessons death teaches us is to value our friends and family." Just as you are sustained by others, you have the opportunity to nourish and sustain others as well. You touch the lives of others; you illuminate their path with your presence and you may touch the lives of those yet to come with your legacy. It is important to plan for the transfer of personal property, but there is also a sacred opportunity to share from the heart in a way that emotionally engages the giver and the receiver.

Each and every one of us will hand down or leave something behind; the question is, what will it be? How will you be remembered? How will you have shared your values, gifts, life experiences, and blessings? Ethical wills are one way to pass on your life lessons, hopes and dreams, and messages of gratitude, love and forgiveness. They contain a written record of the thoughts and feelings that are most important to you. Ethical wills are not new as they were described in the Bible. Initially orally communicated, they have evolved into written legacies, and now may encompass audio, video and compact disc presentations as well. While they are not intended to be legally binding, they often share meaningful aspects of a family's history and traditions. Ethical wills also may be used to communicate important values and blessings which family members wish to record and pass on to future generations.

An ethical will is a gift that may be treasured by both the author and recipients. People who have written one often describe a feeling of clarity, peace of mind, love, gratitude and a sense that their life mattered. People who have received one often describe a feeling of being loved and appreciated as well as an unbreakable bond, a cherished sense of connection to the person who wrote it. Whether you formalize your thoughts and feelings in an ethical will, choose to leave behind personal notes or video diaries, or share your feelings with those you love, take time to express what is in your heart. For your words will become part of your living legacy, a part of you that will be remembered and treasured by those you love. And as those who have traveled the grief journey before you have shared, at the end of life, it is our connection with one another that matters most.

Please remember that before he died, my son Lived! He was special, he was important and he mattered.

-N.M.
On the death of her infant son

Friendship improves happiness, and abates misery, by doubling our joy, and dividing our grief.

-Joseph Addison

Relationship Inventory

Relationships often provide the foundation for a rich and meaningful life. They provide a sense of connection. They help to define who you are, and who you would like to be. Our relationships forever tie us to our family of origin, our family of choice, and our circle of support and companionship.

In times of great joy and great sorrow, it is often your relationships with those around you that provide a sense of comfort, security and well-being. Throughout this book, you have had a few opportunities to look at how you have been supported and comforted by others. Now, it is time to turn the tables and spend some time reflecting upon how you are present to the significant people in your life. Are you a good friend to others? Are you dependable? Do you honor your commitments . . . keep your promises . . . provide comfort and understanding? Are there relationships which you would like to strengthen . . . hurts you would like to forgive . . . connections you would like to reestablish?

In order to keep the relationships in your life healthy and strong, it is a good idea to periodically look at what you give to others and how you can best support and nurture your "circle of support."

Staying Connected (circle your answer)

Do you have close friendships?

     Yes   No

Do you make spending time with friends a priority?

     Yes   No

Do you honor your commitments \ keep appointments?

     Yes   No

To whom are you a good friend?

_____

_____

To whom do you provide support and encouragement?

_____

_____

Are you a mentor to others? Who have you mentored? Are there mentoring opportunities in your life now?

_____

_____

Are you a member of a blended/merged family? How has that affected you?

_____

_____

How would you describe your relationships with your family?

_____

_____

Are you estranged or disconnected from a loved one now? What steps could you take to repair the relationship?

_____

_____

How could you reach out to others in your community to provide friendship and support?

_____

_____

It is the friends you can call up at four A.M. that matter.

-Marlene Dietrich

Choose your friends. Some friends will always be there for you. Others will slowly fade from your life. My husband and I recognized that we changed also. Sometimes others don't know how to deal with the pain we are experiencing. It's okay to build new relationships.

_-N.Z._

Circle of Support

Who can you turn to when you need support and encouragement? Take a few minutes and write down the names of those closest to you, those who have helped in the past, and those who were there for you in times of crisis.

Inner circle: Who mirrors/reflects your core values?

Middle circle: Think of family, friends, coworkers, neighbors and significant others who have provided support.

Outermost circle: Who provided support at critical intersections: clergy, mental health workers, medical team, hospice staff, funeral director, support group members? What resources were available to you when you needed them?

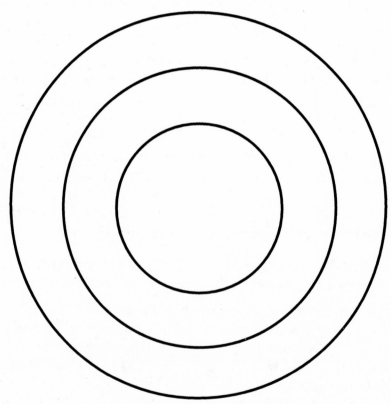

$\mathbb{R}$ Factor: **Relating to Others**

In the last chapter, your relationship to change was discussed. Now, the focus is on your relationship to others. Relationships can bring great joy, as well as great pain. Relationships can fill your life with meaning, happiness, and value, or they can be oppressive and toxic. What do you receive from your relationships: love, friendship, security, safety, support, respect, appreciation? Do you seek physical, emotional and spiritual connections with others? Do your relationships provide a sense of purpose to your life, that is, do they help you feel that you are making a difference in the lives of others and that your unique gifts and talents matter?

While there often are spontaneous moments of connection, generally relationships must be nurtured. Relationships require work, commitment, and take energy to maintain. They also are dynamic in nature and change over time – sometimes growing stronger and other times drifting apart. Sometimes relationships fail. People may be apathetic or ungrateful; they may disappoint you, or betray your trust. Every day you make choices that affect your relationships with others, allowing you to strengthen or weaken your bonds of attachment. Bereaved people often have learned not to take relationships for granted. The death of someone they loved has taught them not only to value life, but that our time here is limited, and that the relationships one forms should be treasured.

One person can make a difference. There is power in one. Each of us must use our gifts. You can do this by doing what you know you must, and being the best that you can be. Sometimes realizing our potential may bring fame and recognition and sometimes it may simply be a quiet contribution to our world. Have you ever been in the presence of someone who makes you feel calmer or safer just by being with them? You might describe it as a caring presence in that these gentle spirits are compassionately and consciously with you, and you feel the moment of connection is sacred.

- When Mrs. B. was dying, her friend was in her hospice room sitting vigil on what was expected to be Mrs. B.'s last night. A hospice volunteer came and offered to keep this friend company. Few words were spoken between the two women, but what was most remembered, was the hospice worker's quiet, comforting, angel-like presence.

- When a Pastoral graduate student was being trained by a hospice mentor, she admired his seemingly natural ability to provide a warm and comfortable presence unlike any she had ever experienced. With his attentive eye contact, his calming voice, and warm affirmations, he made each person he encountered feel truly special.

- Dr. A. was hospitalized with a terminal illness. Realizing that she was nearing the end of her life, she requested that her friend visit her. The friend later described her time with Dr. A. in almost angelic terms. She remembers that Dr. A. had a remarkable calm, and a deeply forgiving heart. The friend felt that rather than tending to Dr. A., she had received the gift of acceptance and compassion. There was a tearful yet sacred energy in the room as the two friends shared a soulful connection.

Relationships can bring out the best in each of us. Your life is shaped by your experiences, including the people in your life who have nurtured and protected you, and taught you valuable life lessons. It is important to honor what others have done for you. And it is equally important to contribute to others by being a positive, healing presence in their lives, too.

We are each of us angels with only one wing, and we can fly only by embracing each other.

-Luciano De Crescenzo

Commitment, unlike attachment, doesn't say 'You must stay a certain way for me to love you.' It says, 'We are in a relationship and I will be there with you through those changes.'

-Joseph Goldstein

Griefstruck

Mr. W. was very devoted to his mother with whom he lived. Acknowledging her age, declining health, and specific wishes, he had accompanied his mother to a local funeral home to prearrange her funeral. Years later, she died at the hospital. He was so distraught that he left his car in the hospital parking lot and walked two miles to the funeral home to announce her death. Even though he had tried to prepare for this moment, when it happened, his grief was so overwhelming that it left him stunned and disoriented. -M.O.C.

Checkpoint

Loss causes you to review your life, what you value, what lessons you learned, what you have accomplished, and what legacy you would like to pass on.

What lessons or phrases did you learn from your great-grandparents, grandparents, and/or parents?

_____

_____

What lessons or phrases did you learn from your siblings/half- or step-siblings?

_____

_____

What lessons or phrases did you learn from your spouse/ significant other?

_____

_____

What lessons or phrases did you learn from your children/ step-children, grandchildren?

_____

_____

What lessons or phrases did you learn from your best friend?

_____

_____

What important things do you want family and friends to know about you?

_____

_____

What is a valuable life lesson that you have learned and would like to share with others?

_____

_____

What are you most proud of?

_____

_____

How would you like to be remembered by others ?

_____

_____

As my mother listened to my grief she revisited the pain of her own father's death – a man she adored and had a close relationship with. Through tears, she reflected on how much she still missed her father and how little time she had to grieve his death. After my grandfather's funeral she immediately resumed her role of managing a household and caring for four children under 10 years of age.

-D.G.

Griefstruck

I prearranged my Mother's funeral ten years before she died. Completing this sacred task with my Mom was challenging, and yet I felt compelled to do it myself. Years later, Mom wrote each of her four adult children a heartfelt letter which we added to her prearrangement file. Toward the end of her life, Mom came to live with us. When she was dying, our family gathered in our home to be with her. Since my sisters came in from out of town, for what would probably be their last visit with Mom, I gave each of my siblings their letter. We read our letters privately, then shared them aloud. My niece read for my sisters who were emotionally overwhelmed. We cried together. I cherish my letter. I am grateful that my Mom gave this gift to me, my sisters and brother.   -M.O'C.

_____

_____

_____

_____

_____

_____

_____

_____

_____

_____

_____

_____

_____

_____
_____
_____
_____
_____
_____
_____
_____
_____
_____
_____
_____
_____
_____
_____
_____
_____
_____
_____
_____
_____
_____
_____
_____

Sudden death leaves the void of no time to say good-by, unfinished business, and unfulfilled dreams. Suicide adds the challenges of social rejection, feelings of guilt and shame, and a struggle to understand "why".

-N.Z.

Depression and Suicide

Depression may be a response to a specific event such as a death or significant loss or it may be the result of a serious illness. If you or a family member are experiencing the symptoms of depression (irritability, sleep disturbances, tearfulness, fatigue, an inability to feel pleasure, feelings of worthlessness, recurrent thoughts of death), it is vital to review your concerns with a health care professional. Medical personnel will be able to monitor your condition, suggest medication if necessary, and provide appropriate referrals.

While sadness is a natural response to loss, and usually does lessen with time, prolonged or extreme sadness requires professional attention. Untreated depression may significantly affect one's quality of life, and in extreme cases, may be a contributing factor to attempted or completed suicides. It is often difficult to comprehend why someone would take his or her own life. Unlike the case in a natural or even accidental death, survivors of suicide (those bereaved people who cared about someone who completed suicide) struggle to understand why someone would choose to end his or her life. While the contributing factors are probably unique to each situation, the impact on family and friends who are left behind may be more universal. Survivors often experience a wide range of emotion from sadness to anger to despair. Survivors may feel dazed, confused, guilty, shamed, rejected, abandoned and, "in most cases," according to Dr. Terry Hargrove, "suicide is experienced by loved ones as an insult to the relationship."

So what do you do if you are a "survivor of a suicide"? Or how do you support a friend, a family member, or co-worker who has experienced a completed suicide in their family? In the course of our work, suicide survivors have shared some personal experiences that they have found to be both helpful and hurtful. In their honor, these suggestions are passed on.

What helps

- Allow the survivors to share their stories. Provide a safe environment in which they may cry or express anger.

- Give the family a chance to tell their story in their own time, and place. Contact other survivors or a suicide survivor's group for information and support.

- Use the name of the deceased when talking to the family – do not assume that by not mentioning the person, they won't be thinking about him or her.

- When appropriate, share positive experiences and memories of the person with the family.

- Be "fully present" to the survivors – sometimes just quietly sitting with them can provide tremendous help and support.

- Look for opportunities to provide practical assistance such as transportation, meals, housekeeping, child or elder care, and companionship as coping with a sudden death often adds to the grief burden.

- If you feel the survivors may be ready, suggest joining a survivors' support group or help them seek out other community resources. Offer to attend a meeting with them to provide additional support.

- Stay in touch. Often most support is available immediately following a death. By keeping in close contact, you will be able to support a friend or family member through some difficult adjustments.

Things to avoid

- Do not judge, criticize, or blame – saying things such as "didn't you know he/she was depressed" or "didn't you see any signs of his/her intentions" can be extremely painful. Avoid clichés such as "his suffering is over" or "perhaps she's at peace now."

- Do not try to deny a survivor his or her tears or anger. Do not minimize, trivialize, or use humor to try to ease the survivor's emotional pain. Listen with compassion but do not try to "take on" or take over a survivor's feelings.

- Do not pry for details – let the family share whatever is comfortable for them.

- Do not gossip, speculate, or "guess" as to the cause – there's rarely one reason.

- Do not "compete" with a survivor's experience or feelings. Do not say you know just how they feel or try to "match tragedies" with your experiences.

- Do not shun, avoid, or exclude friends and family members of the deceased.

I felt the need to share my feelings and experiences following my father's suicide. However, I had to learn to be selective in doing so. Not everyone is comfortable or skilled in handling that type of pain.

-H.G.

Following my son's death, a friend told me: "My daughter had cancer. Your son chose to take his life. My grief is greater than yours." She is still a very close friend today although I felt I had to teach her that it doesn't matter how someone dies . . . the fact that they died is still the cause for the underlying grief.
                                                                    _-N.Z._

If you can learn from hard knocks, you can also learn from soft touches.

-Carolyn Kenmore

Honoring Your Life

Sharing family stories has always been a time-honored tradition. However, in recent years it seems that this activity has become even more popular. Whether family stories are shared through genealogy research, scrapbooking, written or oral histories or the passing down of family keepsakes, what is handed down to future generations becomes an integral part of our living legacy – a critical link between our past and our children's future.

Recently, you may have heard or seen some creative ideas for how families are choosing to record their genealogy, commemorate significant religious or family events, or pass on treasured traditions. Ethical wills are certainly one way to record those things you would like future generations to know about you and your family, but there are many others as well. You may wish to start a dialogue with those who are important to you now as to how you would like to commemorate your family's history and traditions. Here are a few options.

- Create a family photo album or website. Organize it in a way that feels right for your family. Use journaling to capture memorable stories and quotes.

- Place a letter in your prearrangement file at the funeral home, or give it to a trusted friend or family member. Ask that the letters be given to significant people at the time of your death.

- Select photos for a photo board for a celebration of life service, or create your own photo montage.

- Videotape a message for your family.

- Make an audio tape, telling your story, in your own words for your friends and relatives.

- Honor military service. Ask family members who have been in the military to share their experiences with you. Some of these stories may become unique ways to celebrate their life histories.

- Prepare a computer, or slide presentation. (At your request, these presentations also may be used to commemorate your life at your funeral service.)

- Collect linking objects; special mementos that remind you of family members. Display them in your home now. Use them later, at a memory table, to acknowledge the importance of your loved ones.

- Keep a Family Bible – it will become a treasured keepsake as family members receive it.

- Bequeath your diary, journal, book of quotes or humor to someone who you believe will most appreciate it.

- Buy a special present for significant people in your life. Leave instructions that the gifts be distributed upon your death with a personally written note.

The death of someone you love often brings new perspective to the connections you share with friends and family. Recognizing and celebrating these connections is sacred work. Do not get bogged down in trying to make your project perfect, for what is most meaningful to those you love is the effort, not the execution. Keep in mind that you are free to add, change, and redesign your project as your time and energy permits.

Tip: However you chose to celebrate your family traditions, make sure you safeguard your work by making appropriate copies, storing it in a safe place, and taking the necessary steps to preserve it.

When I heard that my father's uncle had died, my wife and I began preparing to attend the out of town funeral. The next day I found out that a funeral service would not be held, per his uncle's request, I felt disappointed and kind of "empty" inside. I wanted to get together with family to share stories, to pay my respect, and to say goodbye to Uncle Ed in a physical sense. I still regret not having that opportunity.

-R.J.G.

My sister died at home, a long way away from me. She had battled cancer for 10 years. She lived in Denver and when she was told the end was near, she came to Chicago to say good-bye to everyone. I drove up from North Carolina to be with her. Two weeks later my family and I drove back for her funeral. She was one of the bravest and most dignified people I have ever known.

-T.McC.

Disenfranchised Grief- The Forgotten Mourner

For some, the pain of a loss is complicated by the additional burden of disenfranchised grief. Dr. Ken Doka, author of <u>Disenfranchised Grief: Recognizing Hidden Sorrow</u>, defines disenfranchised grief as the "grief that people experience when they incur a loss that is not or cannot be openly acknowledged, publicly mourned, or socially supported." Dr. Doka's early work describes three categories of loss that are demonstrated when the relationship, the loss, or the griever is not recognized or supported.

Is disenfranchised grief a part of your loss history? Can you think of a time when you felt your grieving was not recognized by others? Look back at your loss history (Chapter Two) and review your list of people whose deaths impacted you. Were any of them extended family members, ex-spouses, step-children, or step-parents? Have you lost a partner, a close friend, a neighbor, a patient, a client, or co-worker whose death has impacted you greatly? Sometimes it is the emotional bond one feels with a person rather than a biological or legal connection that contributes to a deep sense of loss. And when this sense of loss is not, or cannot, be acknowledged by others, it can inhibit one's ability to mourn and thus may complicate one's grieving.

Another way you may experience this type of grief is when your sense of loss is not understood or accepted by others. Many of us can relate to the deep sorrow of losing a beloved pet and yet often this type of loss does not receive the recognition of other losses. Or perhaps if a loved one died while incarcerated, or as the result of a stigmatized illness or addiction, you may feel you did not receive the same type of support as you would have in other circumstances. Or if you suffered a loss as the result of a miscarriage, stillbirth, or an elective or therapeutic abortion, you may not have had the opportunity to share your loss as publicly with others.

And finally have you experienced losses where you were not acknowledged as a griever due to your age, your physical or mental status, or life circumstances? Oftentimes, children and the elderly are excluded from funeral services by caring family members who feel it is kinder to shield or protect them from the physical and emotional stress of being involved. The same may be true for those friends and family members who have a mental or physical impairment. In some cases, this may be the best decision; however, in others it may deny people who are feeling a loss deeply, the opportunity to give and receive much-needed support. This also may hold true for family members who have experienced a loss while physically separated from family due to work responsibilities, geographical distance, educational commitments, or military service. For these bereaved people, as for all those whose loss was not acknowledged by others, the need may still exist to create their own unique ways to express and release their grief.

Another look...

Take another look at your loss history that you created in Chapter Two. Are there other losses you need to add – losses that perhaps you did not think of or recognize at the time? While it is true that you cannot go back and recapture lost opportunities to mourn your loss, you do have the ability to acknowledge your own disenfranchised grief now. If you find that you feel the need to release grief reactions which you may have suppressed for years, seek healthy ways to do so now. Share your feelings with a trusted friend, a clergy person, or a counselor. Create a ritual which will give you the opportunity to grieve your loss – either with others or alone, depending upon your circumstances and preference. And understand that an important step in releasing disenfranchised grief is to accept and acknowledge it for yourself.

Losing a child to SIDS is a unique crisis. The child dies suddenly, unexpectedly, and for no apparent reason. I was stunned to discover the lifeless infant. There was no adequate explanation.

-D.T.
Daycare provider

_____

_____

_____

_____

_____

_____

_____

_____

_____

_____

_____

_____

_____

_____

_____

_____

_____

_____

_____

_____

_____

_____

_____

_____

_____

_____

_____

_____

_____

_____

_____

_____

_____

_____

_____

_____

_____

_____

_____

_____

When our beloved cat, Sammy, died after 19 years with our family, I felt overcome with grief. He had been such a good friend, such a source of unconditional love, that our house felt quiet and lonely without him. We missed him so much that it hurt to think about him, and yet everything reminded us of him. Slowly, our memories of him became more sweet than sorrowful, but I was surprised at how long it took for our tears to turn into smiles again.

-M.A.G.

Grief in Our Community, Grief in Our World

Grieving in the workplace

Death visits the workplace in many forms. Perhaps you have experienced the direct loss of a co-worker, have attended a visitation service for a co-worker's family member, or have lost work-related friends, associates or contacts. When a death occurs in the workplace, whether it is the result of natural or unnatural causes, how the situation is handled is critical. Though each case will be unique, having a workplace policy and appropriate referral sources to consult is helpful. Oftentimes, these resource guidelines will address the issue from three perspectives: management responsibilities, co-worker reactions, and the needs of the bereaved.

Management's perspective

In recent years, workplace tragedies have raised the awareness of the impact both death and grieving have in a work environment. Through example and education, worker and management alike have come to appreciate the need for effective communication, non-judgmental support, and practical assistance when dealing with this complex issue.

When a death occurs in a work environment, a manager or a member of the personnel staff usually initiates a dialogue with the family. In some cases, the funeral director may be contacted directly by an employer to gather the details of the funeral arrangements so that they may be distributed to employees, as appropriate. Management's accountability to employees must continue as help is provided in such practical ways as clearing out the person's work space, delivering the final paycheck, returning personal belongings to the family, and processing all necessary insurance, financial, and legal documents. Hiring a replacement also should be done with consideration and when possible, even with input from other employees. Temporary help should be considered so as to avoid conflict that arises when people who have a full workload are asked to take on extra responsibilities. Grief counselors and bereavement educators should be made available.

Grief can be costly to business in that it may be difficult for grieving employees to focus. Grief counseling and a supportive attitude by management may help prevent additional losses to the business, such as increased absenteeism and employee resignation. A calm and caring presence may provide reassurance and help de-escalate tension. Providing timely and accurate information, maintaining an open dialogue, mentioning the deceased by name, involving the appropriate employees in decision-making, offering human resources assistance, having a written office policy and crisis intervention plan, and honoring "bereavement days," all are examples of positive actions employers may take to help grieving employees cope with loss.

Co-workers' perspective

For many, a place of employment is like a home away from home; co-workers may feel like extended family members, especially when long hours are required or employees have worked together for many years. Also, as many people today are geographically separated from their biological families, friends and co-workers may become like a second family. It is important for mourners to have a safe place where they can discuss their concerns and feelings, and have professional and/or peer debriefing and support. Cultural, gender, and age-related issues along with various coping strategies may come into play in how individual employees respond to loss. The loss of a co-worker may result in new roles, responsibilities, and relationships. New relationships, groups, and coalitions may form, while others break down, as the grieving employees adapt to their changed environment.

In addition to their primary concerns, co-workers may need help in coping with secondary losses, such as the fear of losing a job, loss of friendships and alliances, and a generalized fear of the unknown. Bereaved employees may fear taking on additional responsibilities, complain about "extra" workloads, or may object to the way management is handling paying tribute to, and eventually replacing, the person who died. Thus, sensitivity and good communication skills are necessary to help employees effectively cope with loss.

The bereaved's perspective

When grieving people return to work following the death of a loved one, the responses of their co-workers may vary. Depending upon individual personalities, cultural norms, communication skills, and the relationship to the bereaved, people may feel uncertain as to how to approach a newly bereaved coworker. Some may fear that if they acknowledge the loss, they may trigger a tearful reaction or hurtful response. On the other hand, if they say nothing, their silence may be misinterpreted as a lack of concern or empathy. Therefore, it is possible that misinformed coworkers may physically avoid a newly bereaved person by turning down a hallway or avoiding eye contact. While this behavior may be hurtful, it is also an opportunity for the bereaved person to let others know how they would like to be treated. Unfortunately, with current privacy guidelines, it may be up to the bereaved to let management and coworkers know what they are comfortable with, what information about the death they would like disclosed, who they would like to be told, and how they would like others to respond to them. If it is comfortable, a bereaved person may want to initiate a dialogue with management and co-workers upon his or her return to work, in effect, modeling the behavior and level of discussion that the worker finds appropriate.

Grieving at school

Students may be confronted by the serious illness or death of a classmate or faculty member. Most likely a school policy is in place, however, it is usually treated as a guideline as each situation is unique and must be handled on a case-by-case basis. Childhood diseases, accidental deaths, alcohol-

or drug-related deaths, suicide and homicide are real world examples which may be encountered in a school environment. Social workers, counselors, nurses and teachers all play a vital role. Teachers should be briefed, asked about their comfort level with this topic, and then given time to talk with their students before a public announcement is made. After proper authorization and verification of information to be released is obtained, a written communication should be sent home with each student. A contact name and number, at the school, should be provided to offer accurate information and to deter rumors. The letter may be written in English as well as another language if appropriate. A page of helpful hints, resources for coping with loss and traumatic events, or other educational material should be included. Specific examples of how to begin a conversation about what happened and how to respond to the feelings that may surface should be detailed. Counseling services also should be made available for students, teachers, and staff.

Grieving in a social environment

Grieving plays a significant role in organizations such as church groups, support groups, retirement homes, nursing homes, and community groups (women's, men's, medical, psychosocial support). Bereavement committees and specialists may be called upon to help staff and members deal with the death. Supportive aftercare activities include participating in a support group, providing a bereavement library, and sending bereavement cards and literature. Also, a memorial fund, scholarship, or tribute may be initiated to honor and remember the person who died.

On a broader scale, another example of social mourning is "collective grief," which is defined as a large group of people mourning a shared loss. Examples of collective grief are most familiar when a well-known leader or a person of notoriety dies. People often feel close attachments with people they may have never met. Perhaps through television, movies, music, or other public venues, a person may develop a sense of connection with, or admiration for, a public figure. When death claims these public figures it is a reminder that life is fragile, death can be unpredictable, and loss will come to us all.

Roadside memorials

Marking the place where a death occurred is a natural human response. People who knew the deceased as well as supportive members of the community, often bring flowers, teddy bears, candles, religious emblems, cards, signs, and other mementos. By laying these items down at the spot where the death occurred, they are in effect, hallowing the ground where the life of a person they cared about was lost. This memorial provides a focus for their grief, and is a tangible testimonial that the person lived and was loved. In the past, these spontaneous memorials may have been removed prematurely by road maintenance personnel. Now, grief experts have educated school, management, and government officials as to their significance and value, thus allowing the memorials to exist indefinitely.

My joy has returned and I again love the beautiful mornings and wonderful people I meet or have relationships with. I think of her often and sometimes get a little depressed but I have started living again. This began to happen on the 6-month anniversary of her death. I had a dream that was really the first dream I remembered since 9/11, and when I interpreted it, I knew it meant that I was ready to get on with my life.

-M.K,
Mother whose daughter died in 9/11/01 tragedy

SUPPORTING BRIDGES

Support System

Along your grief journey, you may discover many opportunities to give and receive support. Look around you, right now. What examples of physical support do you see... a belt, a baby carrier, suspenders, a wall, a roof, a chair, legs of a table?

Now take some time to look through a few magazines, newspapers, cards, mailings you have received and cut out pictures and images that remind you of the support you have received. Have fun with it. Let your imagination take charge. Include examples of things that you might not readily think of as needing to be supported -- a college student, a bungee jumper, a marionette. Paste the images onto the following page, or create a collage of your own. Look at it whenever you need to be reminded of the support you are receiving from others. While the images may make you smile, the montage also will help remind you that as difficult as your grief journey may be at times, you are not alone.

Tip: Once you have completed your collage, you may wish to send a note of thanks or certificate of support to those who have seen you through your most difficult times.

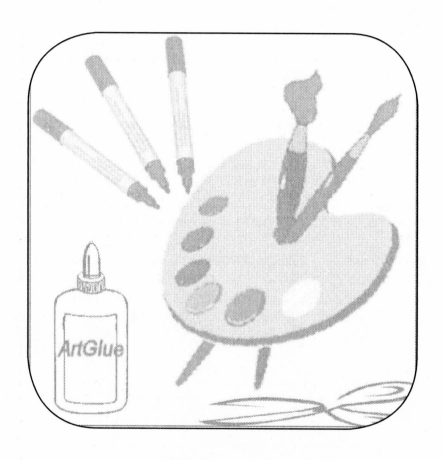

Key Insights

What have I learned about myself?

_____

_____

_____

What have I learned about my
relationship with others?

_____

_____

_____

What have I learned about my loss?

_____

_____

_____

What have I learned about my grief?

_____

_____

_____

Chapter Seven: The Journey Continues

Throughout this bereavnal much has been said about the changes that have undoubtedly come into your life since your loss. As so many bereaved people have shared, following a significant loss, significant changes inevitably occur. So how do you learn to cope with those changes? How do you learn to go on, to find joy and peace and happiness again when you have been so wounded by loss?

For most people, the answer is a little at a time, day by day, week by week, decision by decision. Most likely, whether you are aware of it or not, the process of reconciling your loss, of learning to live in a world without your loved one, already has begun. You, no doubt, are aware of some of the changes you have made. You know that your life, your feelings, your thoughts, hopes, and dreams are all different now. However, what you may not have realized yet is that as you come to accept these "differences," your life is not only being changed, it is being transformed.

Think about the person you have become in the aftermath of your loss. Think about what you have learned – about what you would tell others about coping with loss? As you have read in the experiences of grieving people who have shared their stories, while the pain of their loss often forced them to look at what they lost, the strength of the human spirit also spurred them on to look at what they gained. For some it may have been as simple as a recommitment to spending time with loved ones. For others, it was a reordering of priorities. And for still others, the need to bring meaning and significance to their loss propelled them into accomplishing wonderful things in the memory and commemoration of their loved ones.

Ultimately, what will your response to loss be? As you look at your life now, consider the changes you have made. Recall the important lessons you have learned and know that more discoveries await you. Know too, that just as your grief journey to this point has not been a straight line, the road ahead will not be linear either. Do not be discouraged if you find you are pulled back into your grief by unexpected events or triggers. And do not give up hope if you find yourself experiencing delayed grief reactions. Remember to be patient with yourself, especially if your grief seems to intensify at times as you progress.

Also, keep in mind that people's grief may resurface as they pass through various developmental stages, or attend milestone events. When your loved one died, no matter what the circumstances, you were probably unprepared to accept the permanence of your loss. Whether you dealt well with your initial reactions or not, you must now face a life without your loved one. You may become painfully aware of the absence of your loved one at special occasions, birthdays, graduations, anniversaries, and other significant events. In other words, you must grieve the **lost potential of your relationship**, the loss of unrealized hopes and dreams, the loss of a future together. As one bereaved mother (N.Z.) said, "it hurts to think of those events that I could picture my son being a part of like weddings, births, family parties. No one could take that pain away from me. It's part of my personal grief work and required building up a tolerance for vanished dreams."

As you build up your tolerance for the dreams you may have to release, you will be moving in a positive direction – that is one of transferring your loved one from a physical presence in your life to one of memory. This is a process; one which takes time, patience, and perseverance. Each griever's path is unique and the time it takes to accomplish this task is personal as well. As you find ways to memorialize your loved one within your own heart, family, or community you will be moving forward for this process is not about forgetting your loved one, but about bringing a lasting significance to the life he or she lived.

I still miss Jeffrey. I think of him often and wonder what he'd be like, but now I feel at peace. I believe he is in a better and beautiful place. His death taught me to value each day I have with my family.

-P. M.

Mother whose son died as an infant

Be glad of life, because it gives you the chance to love and to work and to play and to look up at the stars.

-Henry Van Dyke

_____
_____
_____
_____
_____
_____
_____
_____
_____
_____
_____
_____
_____
_____
_____
_____
_____
_____
_____
_____
_____
_____
_____
_____
_____

There is a land of the living and a land of the dead, and the bridge is love.

-Thornton Wilder

$\mathbf{R}$ Factor: Relationship to Spirituality

When you think of your spirituality what comes to mind? Do you think of a connection to a Higher Power, a sense of oneness with others, a shared bond with all living creatures, a feeling of being one with nature, or do you visualize the very best parts of your own being? Do you connect your spirituality with an organized religion, the God of your childhood, or a living presence in your day-to-day existence?

For many people there is a close connection between their spiritual life and a religious affiliation. And for others, there is a vast difference. Traditionally, religion is defined as an organized, external system of beliefs and practices endorsed by a community of fellow believers. It is often associated with specific doctrines, sanctions, controls, clergy, a hierarchy of leadership and a well-defined religious identity. Spirituality, on the other hand, is often used to describe an individual's private search for meaning and connection. While one's spiritual life often includes one's relationship with God, it also may be viewed as an internal connection to the world around us – a sense of belonging to and being part of our universe.

As human beings, each of us has a spiritual nature. As thinking, feeling beings, humans are hard-wired to long for a sense of connection not only with our surroundings, but with something outside of ourselves as well. It is part of our human nature to seek to bring meaning and significance to our living and our dying. Whether you believe that death is simply the end of physical life, or a passage into another form of existence, the reality and awareness of death often prompts a raised consciousness of our spiritual nature. It is certainly paradoxical, but death often causes us to question and explore the meaning and purpose of life.

When a hardship or a death occurs, our sense of spirituality often is challenged. Our pain and sorrow may be expressed as anger - anger which may prompt us to question our spiritual connections. Some people may discount their own spirituality during their time of grieving; others may cling more steadfastly to it seeking comfort, refuge, and relief from their pain. Death has deprived us of an important relationship. Grieving people may feel disconnected from their surroundings, from friends and family members who may not be able to understand or share the depth of their sorrow, so it makes sense that they would seek comfort and connection.

The death of a loved one also may cause grieving people to question their beliefs regarding an afterlife. Some may find comfort in envisioning their loved ones in the presence of a loving God, and others may find peace in their belief in an afterlife or the concept of reincarnation. Regardless of one's beliefs, death remains a mystery for us all. And yet, as it is a fate which each of us will encounter, there is a natural interest in what awaits us beyond this life.

Many books have been written on this subject from various perspectives. From scholars to psychics to people who have survived near death experiences (NDE'S), many have attempted to answer the question of what happens to us when death occurs. What are your personal beliefs regarding an afterlife? How have they influenced your grief journey? Do your beliefs add to your sorrow or do they provide a sense of peace and comfort?

One way to explore your own belief system and perhaps to find a sense of spiritual balance is to go deep inside yourself, to connect with your own inner wisdom. Whether you approach it through prayer, meditation, or quiet solitude, the journey inward is a way to connect with your own intuition, creativity, wisdom, and guidance. If you have not had experience with this type of introspection, you may find it an interesting exercise. You may do it by simply quieting your mind, and allowing your inner guidance to take you where you need to be, or you may want to use one of the many tools designed to help you "go within." From meditation classes to guided visualization tapes to self-help resources there are many tools to help bring a sense of peace and balance to your life.

One such tool which has been used by many cultures to balance spiritual, emotional, and physical well-being is the labyrinth. Gaining popularity once again, a labyrinth is defined as "a structure having numerous intricate winding passages" (Webster's Dictionary).   It is an archetype found in many spiritual traditions.   Centuries old, the labyrinth has come to symbolize the journey inward. Unlike a maze which may have twists and turns, blind alleys, and puzzles to solve, a labyrinth is one clearly defined path, designed to help you find your way. Thus, the challenge becomes not solving the labyrinth, but trusting the path, following the winding course to its center. In other words, **the way in, is the way out.**

Like the grief journey, walking a labyrinth may be seen as a metaphor for the road which takes us into our center and back out to the world. As you progress on your journey toward healing it is a trip you will take, also. While the shock and pain of your loss may have driven you inward, as you heal you will begin to once again connect with the world around you. This journey of insight, self-discovery, and connection is one which you will be traveling for the rest of your life. Like your grief journey it will have stops and starts, sorrows and joys, and moments of chaos and peace.

In many respects, the quality of your life is determined by your experiences, relationships, choices, and attitudes. Feeling balanced, empowered, and spiritually grounded may help you to discover and appreciate the sacredness in your daily life.

Finding the sacred in your grief journey.

- Accept the path you are on. Feel your grief. Cry, scream, and wail if you want to. Realize that you must let your pain in, before you can let it go.

- Reflect on your loss history. Acknowledge the impact of the significant losses in your life.

- Review your relationships. Release negative feelings of anger and guilt. Forgive yourself and others.

- Love and nurture yourself. Practice self-care. Accept help. Establish healthy boundaries. Acknowledge that your choices have consequences.

- Accept loss as an opportunity for growth and healing.

- Live the lessons and legacies of your grief. Walk out of your grief as a changed person. Live your life with love and compassion.

- Honor your divine connection. Trust your path.

- Have gratitude for your relationships with others. Be mindful of the sacredness of life and death. Realize that our humanity connects us to ourselves and each other.

- Receive your gifts. See roadblocks and barriers as teaching tools. Be open to wisdom. Be persistent.

- Embrace your spiritual nature. Nurture your relationship with the Divine.

Accepting that "it can happen to me" was a huge step. Our spiritual lives went through an evolution from religion-based to a true spiritual relationship with God. The search for meaning and purpose becomes apparent and sometimes consuming.

-N.Z.
Bereaved Parent

Griefstruck

The elderly gentleman, who sat across the table from me, lowered his head a bit as he said "You'll probably think I am crazy, I know my kids certainly do." He went on to explain that he had seen his wife, just once, shortly after her death. He was awakened in the middle of the night to see his wife sitting at the foot of their bed. He described her as looking young and beautiful again. He went on to explain that during her long battle with cancer they often would talk about how they were going to fix up their house when she recovered. After her death, he made all of the changes they had dreamed of. The night his wife visited him, she looked around the room at all the improvements he had made in her honor, and smiled. His children felt compelled to try to convince him it was just a nice dream, but he would not deny the healing power of what he saw and felt.

-M.A.G.

_____

_____

_____

_____

_____

_____

_____

_____

_____

_____

_____

_____

Some people have reported experiencing after-death communications (ADC's) with their loved ones. Whether it occurs in the form of a dream, vision or recognizable sign (familiar scent, movement of a significant object, audible sound, etc.) most people find it comforting. As the origin of these encounters is widely debated, the subject remains open to personal belief and dialogue.

Walking Meditation

One of the keys to maintaining a calm and centered sense of self is to find systematic ways to relax and restore the balance between your mind and body. There are many methods available, today, from biofeedback to yoga. Try out a few. Take a yoga class. Listen to a relaxation tape or CD. Pick up a book on meditation or attend an introductory session. You may find that you are especially drawn to one method of relaxation, or that one gives you a greater sense of well-being. Just choose something that allows you to breathe deeply, release muscular tension, and refresh and restore your spirit.

If you would like to try something now, take twenty or thirty minutes and take a walk. Use your intention to relax your mind, release the tensions of the day, and turn inward. Choose an outdoor area such as a park, lake, or quiet street that you find comfortable and pleasant. Center yourself. Give yourself permission to ignore others on the path, so long as you feel safe. Take a deep breath and release it. Tense your body, and then relax. Shake your arms and legs to relax your muscles. Breathe in deeply; exhale fully. Repeat breathing in and out.

Begin your walk. Be aware of your surroundings. Take in nature's wonders. Look up to the sky, down to the ground, and all around. Notice the colors, textures, light, shadows, and fragrances. Feel the sun on your body. Note if there is a soft breeze or gentle wind blowing. Be conscious of your breathing and your movements. Touch something. Watch an animal. Feel your connection to the earth, the planet. Absorb it through your senses. Express your gratitude for being alive and being in this place. Engage all of your senses. Walk for as long as you are comfortable. Return to your beginning with a renewed sense of self and a deeper connection to your surroundings. If your time permits, spend some time journaling about your experiences.

Meditation is simply about being yourself and knowing about who that is. It is about coming to realize that you are on a path whether you like it or not, namely the path that is your life.

–Jon Kabat-Zinn

225

From the heart...

Throughout this bereavnal, you have had the opportunity to share the experiences of other people who have survived loss. If you were to tell another grieving person about your experience of loss, what would you say? Explain how you coped with a difficult or hurtful situation, what or who helped you the most, or what you wish you had known.

Write a letter, poem, or share a memorable experience.

_____

_____

_____

_____

_____

_____

_____

_____

_____

_____

_____

_____

_____

_____

_____

_____

_____

_____

_____

_____

_____

_____

_____

_____

_____

_____

_____

_____

_____

_____

_____

_____

_____

_____

_____

_____

_____

_____

 *Continue to tell the story about your loved one. It creates a natural (and healthy) relationship between you and the deceased that can fuel faith and hope.*

-N.Z.

Seven Gifts of Grief

As you have traveled the grief journey, you undoubtedly have faced many challenges. Some you already may have resolved; some you may be struggling with right now; and others may still lie ahead. Most likely the road has not always been smooth, nor the path always clear; yet like most journeys there is value in the journey itself.

As you have traveled the grief journey, perhaps you already have experienced moments when you became aware of a shift in your attitude, your outlook, or your feelings. For some these are moments of inspiration; for some, they are moments of insight; and for some they are moments of transformation – moments when everything you thought you knew and felt, fall away and something truly beautiful - a special sense of connection and significance - is left in its place.

When these moments of higher consciousness strike, you may begin to see that despite the pain and personal challenges of your grief journey, there are also gifts to be received. Many of the gifts of your journey will be as unique as you are. However, there are some that seem to be shared by many grieving people. Just like most aspects of grief, they do not occur in any specific order, nor within a specific time frame. Yet they are there, like silent signposts along the road, waiting to be discovered by weary travelers.

1) Recognize that you are grieving.

One of the first gifts of your journey may be the opportunity to recognize that your life is different now. Grieving is painful and giving yourself permission to accept that you are doing the hard work of learning to live without someone you love is affirming. Let others know that you are wounded, that you are facing the many challenges of your grief, and allow them to comfort and support you.

2) Reflect on your loss history.

Your loss history is uniquely and authentically yours. It affects every aspect of your life and has contributed to who you are and how you see the world. Taking time to think about the losses you have experienced, and the impact they have had on your life, your outlook, and your disposition can provide both insight and inspiration for your grief journey.

3) Respect your relationships.

Grieving offers you the opportunity to honor past relationships, nurture present ones, and build future relationships. Often when a death occurs, personal roles and responsibilities change. Some relationships may be challenged and others may become more treasured as support and comfort are drawn from them. As many bereaved people have shared, losing someone you love, often makes you cherish your remaining relationships even more.

4) Reestablish healthy boundaries.

For many, grieving is a time of disorganization and daily challenges. Nothing feels or seems normal. During this time, it is easy to forget about taking care of your own physical, emotional, and spiritual needs. Thus, it is important that you make it a priority to establish, or reestablish personal boundaries in order to take care of your own needs. Protect your physical body and immune system by practicing self-care. Eat well-balanced, nutritious meals, get plenty of rest, and give yourself time to relax and renew your mind and body.

5) Realize the transformative power of your grief.

Grief offers opportunity for transformation. The ability to move beyond adversity and to discover specific ways in which your loss might be a catalyst for positive change is challenging. Awareness of your inner guidance as you do your grief work may lead to the path of wisdom and compassion, which will enrich your life, as well as those around you.

6) Review your priorities; live consciously.

Grief reminds you that your time each day is limited and that the people you love should be respected and cherished. Living consciously means having a heightened awareness of your goals and purpose, and actively managing your time and relationships in that context.

7) Rediscover the sacredness of life and death.

Being present when a life comes into or departs from our world is often described as sacred. There is an element of mystery, as well as a sense of the divine, associated with both transitions. Life and death add value to your core being, and they imprint how you relate in the world.

Remember: You are a lifelong learner. Each day provides new opportunities to use or squander your gifts and to appreciate or exploit the gifts of others. Acknowledging each person's unique gifts is a way of recognizing their intrinsic value.

 **Checkpoint**

One of the many changes you may have noticed after your loss is a deepened sense of spirituality or spiritual connection. Contemplating spiritual questions and confronting our spiritual beliefs, conflicts, and commitments may help us reframe or recommit to our life purpose and priorities.

Consider specific ways in which your sense of spirituality may have been challenged or confirmed by your loss.

1. What do you hold sacred?

_____

_____

2. What are your beliefs regarding an Afterlife?

_____

_____

3. How are you more compassionate to yourself and others?

_____

_____

My sense of family was profoundly affected. I wanted, and still want, to be with them often. Life is brief and each of us is here for a short time, so I'm evaluating how I want to use my time.

-S.N.
On the death of her 19-year old nephew

4. How have your relationships changed since your loss?

_____

_____

5. How are your priorities now different?

_____

_____

6. What is different about your attitude or disposition since your loss?

_____

_____

7. How would you describe your sense of spiritual connection?

_____

_____

8. What do you consider your life purpose to be? How are you fulfilling it in your daily life?

_____

_____

My volunteer work is very important to me. I enjoy spending time with people and I am happy I have the opportunity to help others.

-R. T.

One definition of spirituality is transcendence — to go beyond ourselves —beyond what we thought we were.

-Adina Wrobleski

The Gifts of Your Journey

What are the gifts of your unique grief journey? As you think about the lessons you have learned from your grief, and the changes you have made since your loss occurred, write a word or two in each of the "presents" below, to signify the gifts you have received.

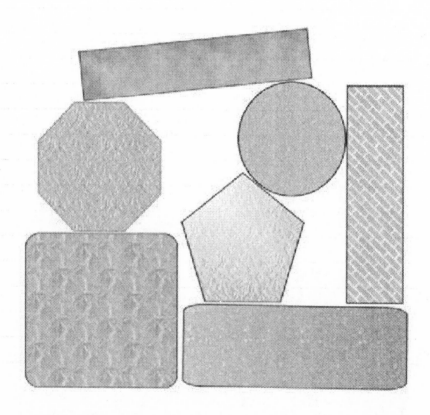

The lessons of shared grief can be profound. My mother and I emerged from our individual grief knowing one another more fully and loving one another more deeply.

-D.G.

Sharing Your Gifts

Grief and spiritual connection are personal journeys, but neither you nor others must travel alone. There are times for solitude, but also times for sharing. As a griever who has been down the path, you know there are other people in your world who are also grieving losses of their own. You know what was helpful for you. Now may be the time for you to reach out to others to help lighten their load.

Who do you know who might be struggling with loss?

_____

_____

What could you do, today, this week, or soon to help ease their pain? Use your own ideas or try one of the following.

- Call or send an e-mail.
- Write a personal note or card.
- Offer practical assistance such as a homemade meal or transportation.
- Accompany them to a support group.
- Invite them out for a cup or coffee, a movie, or lunch.
- Pay a personal visit.
- Buy a small gift and drop it off or mail it.
- Share resources.

You never know how an act of kindness or consideration may affect someone. Sometimes the smallest of gestures may have great consequences. There are countless stories of how one act of kindness gave someone hope, changed someone's destiny, or perhaps even saved a life. Reach out to others with kindness and compassion and you are sure to enrich your life as well.

Today we are building new dreams — not like the ones we once envisioned. But "new" in the sense that we are taking chances, doing things we never thought about doing, helping others in ways we never imagined, and concentrating on who we are and what our purpose really is.

-N.Z.

Sacred Space

If you do not already have one, consider creating a sacred space for yourself in your home environment. It can be designed around a comfortable chair, the corner of a room, a shelf, a favorite spot in your garden, or anyplace that you can surround yourself with things that comfort and uplift your spirit. It can become your place to read, listen to music, meditate, pray, worship, grieve, journal, paint, or simply be alone with your own thoughts and feelings.

You can decorate your sacred space with things that inspire you and bring you joy – fresh flowers, candles, photographs, statues, art, soft fabrics, incense, altar cloths, pictures, pillows, sacred objects, and gifts from nature such as shells, rocks, leaves and driftwood. You can add things that remind you of the loved ones you have lost or choose to honor their memory somewhere else. All that is important is that this space be meaningful to you and filled with objects you find comforting. Once you have begun creating your sacred space, spend time there – every day. Even if you only have the opportunity to spend fifteen minutes there, make an appointment with yourself and keep it.

Get started now. Write down some of the items you would like to bring into your sacred space.

_____

_____

_____

_____

_____

_____

To be spiritual, then, is to take the energy of the spirit and direct it to commitments and connections, to personal development, or to that which is perceived as the ultimate.

-Rollo May

Looking back

As you began this journey through your grief, you completed the following exercise. Do it again, today. Congratulate yourself for the positive changes you have made. Celebrate your growth. Take comfort in how far you have traveled.

Today I...

Feel like this:

Look like this:

Express yourself: Use your creativity to express your feelings. You may use photographs, draw stick figures, cut out magazine images, write key words or phrases, or use colored markers to represent your thoughts and feelings.

The world is round and the place which may seem like the end may be only the beginning.

-Ivy Baker Priest

Life is change. Growth is optional. Choose wisely.

-Karen Kaiser Clark

Death is a good friend, an awfully good friend, because it tells us we don't have forever, and that to live is now; therefore, you see how precious every minute is.

-Leo Buscaglia

Lessons Learned

Revisit your Key-Insights answers from Chapters One through Six, and write your most meaningful responses below.

What have I learned about myself?

_____

_____

_____

What have I learned about my relationship with others?

_____

_____

_____

What have I learned about my loss?

_____

_____

_____

What have I learned about my grief?

_____

_____

_____

A Final Note

Several years ago, a mutual friend thought we should meet because we shared a passion for our work in the area of death, dying and bereavement. She introduced us, and that meeting proved the beginning of a friendship which has flourished over time. Today, we are close friends, co-founders of GrieForum, and now co-authors. This book also reflects our personal journeys for from its inception to its final production, we too have traveled a road of self-examination, self-discovery, growth, and transformation. In the years it took to complete this book, we have experienced many of the losses discussed within it both personally and through the eyes and experiences of our friends, family members, and clients.

We are grateful for the lessons we have learned during these encounters with grief for they have added to our collective understanding of what it means to be griefstruck. It has been our privilege and honor to accompany bereaved people on their personal journeys through grief. Each day we are challenged and blessed by the sacredness of our work.

We hope that you, too, have found the sacredness in your grief journey. We feel honored that you have chosen to include us, in some small way, as companions. We believe that death is much more than an ending, and that in a very real sense it does give those who are left behind, the opportunity to rebuild, or reshape their lives in ways that bring both meaning and commemoration to those who have died. It is our hope that you will integrate the lessons you have learned, and those you will continue to learn, into your life in ways that will help you to transcend the pain of your loss, and transform the sadness of your grief.

-Mary Ann & Marguerite

REFERENCES AND RESOURCES

Doka, Ken, ed. (2002), <u>Disenfranchised Grief</u>
<u>New Directions, Challenges, and Strategies for Practice.</u>
Research Press, Champaign, IL

Figley, Charles, Bride, Brian, Mazza, Nicholas, ed., (1997),
<u>Death and Trauma.</u> Taylor and Francis, Washington, D.C.

Heinlein, Susan, Brumett, Grace, Tibbals, Jane-Ellen (1997),
<u>When a Lifemate Dies.</u> Fairview Press, Minneapolis, MN

Kubler-Ross, Elisabeth (1969), <u>On Death and Dying.</u>
Collier Books, Macmillan Publishing Co., New York, NY

Myss, Caroline (1997), <u>Why People Don't Heal and How
They Can.</u> Three Rivers Press, New York, NY

Prend, Ashley Davis (1997), <u>Transcending Loss</u>
<u>Understanding the Lifelong Impact of Grief and How to Make
It Meaningful.</u> Berkley Books, Penguin Group, New York, NY

Rando, Therese (1988), <u>How to Go On Living When
Someone You Love Dies.</u> Lexington Books, Lexington, MA

Wolfelt, Alan (2004), <u>When Your Pet Dies</u>
<u>A Guide to Mourning, Remembering and Healing.</u> Companion
Press, Fort Collins, CO

Wrobleski, Adina (1994), <u>Suicide Survivors:</u>
<u>A Guide for Those Left Behind.</u> Afterwords. Minneapolis, MN

3 1191 00815 0591

Notes